Jnana Sankalini

Tantra

Lord Shiva revealing the secrets of Tantra to Parvati

The author being blessed by his Master

Jnana Sankalini

Tantra

PARAMAHAMSA PRAJNANANANDA

Jnana Sankalini

Tantra

First Edition 2004

Paperback ISBN 3-902038-18-7
Hardbound ISBN 3-902038-20-9

Published by: **Prajna Publication** Diefenbachgasse 38/6, A-1150 Vienna

British Library Cataloguing in Publication Data
A catalogue record of this book is available from the British Library

Printed and distributed by Sai Towers Publishing, Bangalore.

DEDICATION

To the memory of my beloved Guruji, source of knowledge, infinite compassion and love, who taught me by his living example the qualities a teacher should cultivate and blessed me by making me a recipient of his wisdom.

May this work be a reflection of his teaching, and prove a valuable tool along the road of self-enquiry.

With boundless love,

Prajnanananda

ACKNOWLEDGEMENT

This book was the patient work of many years. No good work is accomplished without cooperative effort and the blessings of God and Gurus. My sincere love and appreciation to one and all who have helped me in various ways to bring out this book.

God will bless them,

Prajnanananda

CONTENTS

PART I

Introduction to Jnana Sankalini Tantra

The Vedic Culture

When I was a young boy, living in a village in India, I came across a few practitioners of Tantra, known as tantrics. They wore distinctive red clothing, their bodies were smeared with ashes, supposedly collected from the cremation ground, their foreheads were lined with vermilion and they carried a *damaru* or tabor in their hand as well as a trumpet-shaped horn. Their eyes seemed to be permanently blood-shot and they wore rosaries around their necks, some even carried human skulls. Their ferocious appearance created fear in the minds of innocent people, especially small children, and many stories were told about their supernatural powers.

Later in life I had the opportunity to meet some well-trained tantrics and was impressed with their practices and achievements. After I met my Gurudev many of my former doubts on Tantra disappeared. Under his guidance, I had the rare opportunity to study some of the tantric texts and delve into the corresponding scriptures with a meditative outlook.

My beloved Gurudev taught me that life is an opportunity to manifest love, harmony, and peace. The combination of these qualities is known as divinity, and all religions and spiritual paths are designed to manifest this divine nature and help each individual reach the highest stage of realization.

The Vedas are a storehouse of spiritual wisdom with no known individual authorship. The ancient *rishis*, by contemplation and meditation, handed down this sacred knowledge through oral tradition to enrich the spiritual life of generation after generation. The Vedic culture of spirituality and wholesome living predates recorded history and takes into account every aspect of human life including our overall physical, emotional, intellectual, and spiritual development.

At a later period Sage Vyasa compiled the Vedas and edited them into four major parts: Rig, Yajur, Sama, and Atharva or

Atharvana. These four Vedas became the source of various philosophical traditions and scriptures in India. *Rig* comes from the root word *richa*, which means 'to pray' or 'to speak.' The Rig Veda is the art of praying outwardly and inwardly. *Yuj* means 'to be united with divinity' and *yaj* is 'to worship.' The Yajur Veda therefore, unites the seeker with divinity in holy worship. The Sama Veda brings all round harmony in every step of life while Atharva or Atharvana Veda (the source of Tantra) teaches us how to reach the ultimate goal of life through other means. The Vedas are also divided into two major sections:

karma kanda or the Path of Action,
jñana kanda or the Path of Knowledge.

Every individual has immense spiritual potential waiting to be tapped through either of these paths otherwise known as *nigama.* These sacred texts lead a devotee towards the attainment of perfection and the manifestation of one's inherent divinity. The Path of Action is extremely elaborate and systematic. It involves many ritualistic practices that help a seeker to achieve inner purification. The Path of Knowledge contained in the last part of the Vedas is also known as Vedanta or the Upanishads and highlights the philosophical and intellectual understanding of life itself and the goals to be achieved through self-enquiry and meditation.

The fourth Veda or Atharvana was revealed in order to make the ritualistic practices simpler and more readily accessible to the average person. One of the particular disciplines that the Atharvana Veda sets out is known as Tantra.

The Vedas include the two notions of *nigama* and *agama,* both words go back to the root verb *gam,* which means 'to go,' 'to acquire,' or 'to obtain.' Both paths are intended to help human evolution and uncover the spiritual treasure hidden within each human being. In time, Tantra evolved as a distinct spiritual practice with its own texts, scriptures, interpretations, and teachers.

The Science of Tantra

The Vedas, otherwise known as *nigama*, are considered the compilation of all knowledge. From this sacred source emanates the science of Tantra, which is also called *agama.* The Vedas describe ways to obtain knowledge, whereas the Tantras emphasize sincere practice.

Tantra is a universal method or practice (sadhana) developed to bring God into our life and can be followed irrespective of any religion. Tantra has endured much notoriety and has been misused because of wide misinterpretation and emphasis on the ability to acquire occult powers. Without the proper understanding of the nature and mode of practice, these abilities are usually used merely to procure elusive enjoyment and can be short lived. In reality Tantra is a highly regulated and disciplined path. Tantric practices were not only developed to address the minor misfortunes and practicality of everyday life, but to ultimately help the seeker gain spiritual enlightenment and Self-realization.

āgataṃ śiva vaktre ca gataṃ ca girijā śrutau
mataṃ ca vāsudevasya tenāgama iti smṛtah

"That which proceeds from the mouth of Shiva and enters into the ears of Girija (Parvati or Shakti) and that which is the opinion of Vasudeva is known as *agama.*"

In this way the supreme knowledge of Lord Shiva, taught to Parvati for the purpose of self-evolution, is known as *agama.*

sarvārtha yena tanyante trāyante ca bhayāt janān
iti tantrasya tantratvaṃ tantrajña paricakṣate

"It is Tantra, as described by its masters, that bestows all goals and liberates a person from all fear."

Human life is burdened by hurdles and difficulties. Every individual seeks to be rid of trouble, disease, and worry. With a proper focus and an attitude of non-attachment, any problem can be overcome. Mastering the science of Tantra helps to diminish suffering and eventually reach liberation. The practice of Tantra incorporates three aspects:

1) Ritualistic practices,
2) Esoteric, meditative practices,
3) A philosophical outlook towards life.

The guru knows, according to the individual makeup and capacity of each student, what steps or techniques will best hasten one's spiritual evolution. The teachings are imparted with the disciple's highest good in mind and consist of very precise analyzed methods that should be followed exactly as they are taught. The disciple is given the tools or technology necessary to achieve the highest stage of realization. Tantra claims that through sincere effort and the strongest desire, liberation is possible within a single human lifetime.

Definitions of Tantra

The word Tantra can be interpreted in several ways. It is originally derived from the root verb *tan*, which means 'continuation,' 'diffusion,' and 'expansion.' Its practice is designed to expand spiritual experience and acquire a higher level of consciousness. Another root of Tantra is *tantr*, which means 'to rule,' 'to govern,' 'to control,' 'to perform,' and 'to keep in order.' In this way, through a disciplined and highly regulated spiritual life, Tantra is a means to expand individual consciousness into universal consciousness.

tvam atra tatra sarvatra iti tantra

"O God! You are here, there, and everywhere, such experience is Tantra."

A highly advanced spiritual seeker is able to experience God in all and all in God. Only a tranquil mind with a universal outlook can grasp this state.

sarva jñānarāji vistāreṇa vistṛṇoti
yat śāstraṃ tat tantra śāstram

"The scripture of Tantra is such that it enables one to widen the periphery of knowledge."

Knowledge is strength and brings a seeker to the door of liberation. Knowledge, in tantric terms, is the result of action and becomes the seed of supreme love. Once this seed is implanted in the heart of a suitable person it is ever expanding. Another definition of Tantra is that it is the art of gaining freedom from the cage of the three bodies. Each human being, i.e., the soul, is the child of God housed in a shrine, the body temple. The body is not one but three: gross (physical), astral (mind), and causal (ignorance). Through the practice of a spiritual life, filled with devotion, a devotee can obtain detachment from one's body and experience the latent divinity already existing within. The soul's journey is from the un-manifested stage to the manifested stage and then back again to the un-manifested stage.

tanu traya tāraṇa iti tantra

"The state of freedom from attachment to the three bodies."

tam trāṇa karoti iti tantra

"Tantra is the scripture of liberation."

Ignorance is the cause of suffering and attachment. Knowledge brings liberation because it dispels the darkness of ignorance. Expansion (*tan*) and contraction have to do with the breath and are correlated to life and death respectively. Narrowness in mind, heart, and expression is the cause of suffering, while expansion in love and understanding leads to abiding peace and liberation. Breath is the external manifestation of life. In every disposition your breath changes. A normal breath is every four seconds. Extreme emotion makes you gasp or pant. Rapid breathing, at an interval of one to five every two seconds, portrays strong emotion such as anger and passion, which only lead to suffering. When the duration of the breath is prolonged and expanded, inner peace and calmness can be achieved. If *tan* means 'expansion,' *trana* means 'liberation,' so *tantra* is a path to liberation through expansion or prolongation of the breath. This facilitates an amplified capacity to understand the deeper meaning of life.

The common goal of all religions is addressed in different terms. In Hinduism it is known as *moksha*, in Buddhism it is called nirvana, and in Christianity it is thought of as entering the Kingdom of Heaven. Nirvana, in Sanskrit, is translated as extreme tranquility leading to a breathless state. In the Gospel of John, Jesus says God should be worshipped "in spirit and truth." In Latin, 'spirit' can also mean 'breath.' In other words, the Kingdom of Heaven is to be experienced within through breath-control and self-discipline. To attain the universal goal of abiding peace and happiness and liberation, it is necessary to use the tantric tool of expansion through breath regulation. Tantra provides a method by which the breath can be expanded to hasten spiritual evolution. A normally active, healthy individual breathes an average of 21,600 times a day. Through a disciplined lifestyle and the art of breath-control, this can be reduced to 2,000 times a day. My own beloved Guruji, Paramahamsa Hariharananda, repeatedly instructed,

"Breath control is self-control.
Breath mastery is self-mastery.
Breathless stage is deathless stage."

Tantra is a *sadhana*, which employs a systematic step-by-step approach with a rigorous physical and psychological discipline that brings about the over-all development of the individual. Tantra is not only a spiritual discipline but it is also a regulated path, open to all religions, that seeks to bring God into every day life by developing a universal outlook.

Misinterpretation through the Ages

With the passage of time, the real meaning of Tantra and tantric practices has been widely misunderstood. As it was handed down through the ages, a myth based on misconception began to spread. Tantra was believed to be a secret art for acquiring magical and occult powers and was demeaned as just a tool for prolonging the capacity of enjoyment through the senses. It was commonly believed that tantrics did not lead a self-disciplined life because their primary goal was self-gratification. They were accused of having supernatural powers and using hypnotism to obtain whatever they desired. Tantra is scientific, there are no more magical elements in it than in any other discipline; e.g., electricity would appear magic to a man living in the Stone Age.

Erotic imagery on early Indian temples has perplexed scholars and historians for centuries. The male-female union form as seen in temple walls, sculptures, and paintings in caves in India is not erotic art. Yet if seen only at the ordinary level of understanding, this image might seem to confirm so many of the longstanding misperceptions about Tantra as evidence of a practice that incorporates sexuality into worship. Nothing could be further from the truth. The form represents the manifestation of the highest spiritual attainment as the union of consciousness with God or the Absolute.

As a spiritual discipline it has a lot more to offer than meets the eye. The Sadhana Shastra (practical spiritual text) handed down from the Vedas provides a vast scope of learning, a deep understanding of life, and practical steps for leading a life of self-discipline in order to attain Self-realization. Tantra was misinterpreted because such symbolic teaching, full of deep inner meanings and metaphorical connotations, cannot be fully understood without the help of a true guide. Scanty knowledge and literal interpretation always produces poor results, and Tantra has suffered at the hands of misguided people, willing to believe that as a spiritual science, it is much less than it really is.

Consciousness and Energy

Shiva is the most important aspect of the Hindu trinity. From the Vedic period, Lord Shiva is worshipped as the bestower of liberation and the source of all knowledge.

jñānaṃ maheśvarāt ichhet

"Seek knowledge from Shiva."

The Parshurama Kalpasutra, a treatise on spirituality and Tantra, highlights Shiva's role as the master of knowledge:

bhagavāna parama śiva bhattāraka śrutyādi aṣṭādaśa vidyāh
sarvāni darśanāni līlaya tattadavasthāpanaḥ praṇīya samvinmayā
bhagavatyā bhairavyā svātmavinnay'a pṛstah pancabhih mukhaih
pancāmnāyaṃ paramārtha sārabhūtaṃ praninàya

(Sutra 2)

"Lord Parama Shiva Bhattaraka teaches eighteen *vidyas* including the Vedas, which are all branches of philosophy with a logical approach, to Parvati. Bhairava, with his five mouths, symbolize the five paths essential for the improvement of the life of others."

Shiva is considered the master of the eighteen *vidyas,* which are branches of classical knowledge and include: Phonetics, the Science of Language, Ritual, Prosody (verse forms and poetic meters), Astronomy, Etymology, Investigation (Mimamsa), Logic, History (Purana), Ethics (Dharmashastra), Medicine, the Science of War, Fine Arts, Politics (Niti Shastra), and the four Vedas (Rig, Yajur, Sama, and Atharva). Shiva is the illustrious master of Tantra, Yoga, Music, and Knowledge. Through his guidance he enables the spiritual seeker to attain inner perfection and ultimately liberation.

In all mythological descriptions Shiva is a householder yogi and lives with his divine consort, Parvati and their two sons Ganesha and Kartikeya. In tantric practices both Shiva and Parvati are worshipped together, since the former represents consciousness and the latter, in the form of *shakti,* symbolizes energy. In tantric meditation, inner bliss can be obtained by arousing latent energy in the body temple and uniting it with Shiva. Tantra uplifts consciousness in order to embrace the cosmic spirit.

Since energy or *shakti* is feminine in nature, tantrics worship the Divine Mother. A mother's love is unconditional and she has a pivotal role in the child's existence. A baby is nurtured and thrives under her care. Whatever is learned during the early stages of life from the mother or a 'mother figure,' will stay imprinted in the child's memory for life. Tantra's objective is to evoke a mother's love in the mind of the aspirant so as to stimulate the heart's natural love and transform that inert energy into dynamic kinetic energy. Shakti (Parvati) and Lord Shiva can then join in a state of supreme union.

Tantric Literature

There are approximately 192 known tantric texts available. Aryavarta or mythological India was divided, according to tantric belief, into three regions, each responsible for sixty-four Tantras. The first region, Rathakranta, ran from the Vindhya Mountains in Central India all the way to Rameshvara in the South. The second region, Ashvakranta, extended from Uttarakhanda (the Himalayas) to the Vindhyas stretching all the way to the East (Bengal and Assam). The last region, Vishnukranta, covered the other side, extending from Uttarakhanda to the Vindhyas, all the way to the Western provinces of Rajastan and Gujarat.

Most tantric texts are still unpublished, but many original manuscripts have been preserved in the British Library and the Library for Oriental Studies in Kolkata, India. Tantric texts are broadly classified into two separate sections:

1) The *Yamala,*
2) The *Damara.*

The Yamala Tantra contains the secret conversations between different deities and their respective consorts. The word *yamala* literally means 'twins,' 'united,' or a 'couple.' The Yamala Tantra includes texts on Rudrayamala, Vishnuyamala, Brahmayamala, Lakshmiyamala, Umayamala, Skandayamala, Adityayamala, and Bhairavayamala, among many others.

The Damara Tantra is dedicated to Lord Shiva and his mystical teachings. *Damara* has several meanings, it stands for 'goblin' or 'an attendant of Shiva,' but it also means 'wonder.' The Damara Tantra includes Yogadamara, Shivadamara, Durgadamara, Sarasvatadamara, Gandharvadamara, Brahmadamara, and many more.

At the start of worship during Hindu ritualistic practices, the five principal deities *pancha devata puja* (Ganapati, Durga, Surya, Shiva, and Vishnu) are mentioned in sequence. Based on this tradition, five groups of tantric texts, associated with these five deities, were developed:

1) The Ganapatya Tantra is associated with Ganapati and Lord Ganesha;
2) The Shakta Tantra is related to Devi, in the form of Durga and Kali;
3) The Saura Tantra is related to Surya, the sun god;
4) The Shaiva Tantra concerns Shiva or Mahakala Bhairava, also known as Shaivagama Samhita;
5) The Vaishnava Tantra is about Vishnu, Krishna, Gopala, and others, as in Pancharatra.

There are many tantric texts belonging to the Buddhist tradition particularly Tibetan Buddhism, where they are referred to as the Apocalyptic or Tantric Vehicle, or Vajrayana. Many of these texts are attributed to the teachings of Shakyamuni Buddha. Worship is dedicated to Tara Devi, a tantric goddess, and there is a predominant use of mantras as well as other ritualistic practices. These texts include the Manjucrimulakalpa, the Guhya Samaja Tantra, the Songs of Milarepa, the Caryagitas, and others.

Integration between the Vedas and Tantra

Tantra respects the dictum of the Vedas and provides a physical, psychological, and spiritual discipline, in the form of *sadhanas*, to accomplish this higher purpose. Historically, Vedic study and practices became restricted to a selected group of people, namely, priests and the elite class. Tantra had the advantage of remaining more universal and accessible to anyone wanting spiritual progress. Tantra puts no bar on caste, gender, or religious belief. It is the shared overall goal of what is the upliftment of the individual in order to embrace the cosmic spirit.

The Vedas and Tantra are considered complimentary to each other. In revered scriptures such as the Mahabharata and the Bhagavatam, there are descriptions of Tantra, underlining its benefits for the attainment of Self-realization. Tantra contains a vast field of spiritual wisdom with elaborate instructions on how to live a spiritual life, and through the implementation of mental and physical discipline, achieve *moksha* or liberation. Tantra provides a pragmatic approach combined with a firm philosophical foundation. It is a systematic step-by-step evolutionary process.

The four main *padas* (steps) of Tantra are the following:

1) *Jñanapada* or the path of Self-knowledge,
2) *Yogapada* or the path of self-discipline,
3) *Kriyapada* or the path of spiritual practice,
4) *Caryapada* or the path of spiritual evolution.

Jñanapada or the step towards Self-knowledge highlights the philosophy of Tantra and the metaphysics which uphold the entire structure. Tantra is a beautiful combination of Vedantic truth and *samkhya* (scriptural) principles. *Jñanapada* points the way for the spiritual seeker to reach the highest goal of life, the experience of divine love and liberation, through understanding and contemplation.

Yogapada includes *sadhanas* or 'spiritual disciplines,' which give sacred knowledge its practical meaning. Yoga is the application of

Vedanta, enabling the *sadhaka* (seeker) to attain divine communion with the Supreme Self. Yoga and Tantra are closely correlated. While Yoga brings harmony in life and union with the Divine, Tantra accelerates this process through a more pragmatic understanding. Yoga and Tantra both utilize the chakras and similar techniques such as *mudras* (posture or gesture of body and hands) and *pranayama* (breath regulation). The most powerful technique Yoga and Tantra have in common is to waken the *kundalini*, or the latent spiritual energy, which lies untapped in every human being.

Kriyapada covers any form of community worship in sacred places, pilgrimages, sacrifices, and fire rituals. Its deeper meaning, however, is to perform every activity in God-consciousness. Every action in the external world, whether within the family, in the confines of society, or in the midst of natural surroundings, is considered *Kriya*. To evolve spiritually, harmony must be incorporated in every aspect and activity of life. *Kriya* combines a spiritual outlook with pragmatic behaviour.

Caryapada, derived from the word *carya,* means to observe personal discipline in daily life. A code of conduct is established, serving as a model for all spiritual aspirants and covering every activity from morning until night. There are additional rituals practiced at specific times during the day, and throughout the calendar year. This step also dwells on such topics as the process of creation, the nature of evolution, and the transmission of the different modes of speech from *para* (supreme thought), to *pashyanti* (cognition), to *madhyama* (intermittent thought process), until *vaikhari* or the audible word is spoken.

Caryapada also teaches *akshara tattva* or the philosophy of letters. It disseminates knowledge on the practical use of mantras (sacred syllables) and the symbolism behind *yantras* (geometric symbols). Additionally, it offers guidance on principles relating to different deities and gives instruction on diverse modes of worship and meditation. *Caryapada* is a treasure chest of valuable guidance and information, and it has been aptly named the path of spiritual evolution.

The Sacred Trilogy

The Hindu Trinity consisting of Brahma, Vishnu, and Shiva, represents creation, sustenance, and dissolution. All of life's activities correspond to these three aspects of creation. Past, present, and future are also associated with creation and its subsequent phases of manifestation and destruction. The principal scriptures of Hinduism are the Trayi Veda or Three Vedas: Rig, Yajur, and Sama. There are also three modes of expression: song, poetry, and prose, as well as three paths for spiritual evolution: karma or action, *jñana* or knowledge, and *bhakti* or devotion. The Prasthana Trayee is a beautiful combination of three sacred texts, the Gita, the Brahmasutras, and the Upanishads, which propound spiritual evolution.

Vedic, yogic, and tantric literature incorporates three levels of language: *loukiki* or traditional, *sahitya* or literal, and *tattviki/ samadhi* or metaphorical. The guidance of a qualified guru is absolutely essential in order to understand the inner meaning of the scriptures, as only through rigorous training in addition to deep contemplation can the hidden message be accurately deciphered.

Tantric texts tend to be very complex and are often misleading when they are taken literally. Some concepts have been perverted and exaggerated resulting in only sensuous interpretations, but Tantra hides many spiritual truths, which remain unrevealed to those who only float on the surface. Tantra, as it has often been interpreted in the West, with the wrong emphasis on sexuality, has been grossly deformed and considerably diminished as a scriptural source of wisdom.

Tantric practices integrate three concepts known as *yantra, mantra,* and *tantra,* which need to be fully understood, literally, mystically, and metaphysically, before plunging deeper into the subject.

The word *yantra* comes from the root verb *yam,* meaning 'to subdue,' 'control,' or 'eliminate.' The word itself is usually interpreted as an instrument or tool used for a special purpose. In ritualistic worship Hindus draw geometrical shapes, engraving them on prescribed metals (copper, silver, or gold) or stone. One common shape is the triangle; with the apex pointing upwards it represents the male aspect and one pointing down represents the feminine. The union of the two, formed by superimposing them, is a hexagon or six-pointed star. Devotees also use coloured powder to draw exquisite designs on the floor, a sand surface, a piece of paper, or even a leaf.

The word *yama* is derived from the same root verb. In the Yoga Sutras of Patañjali, *yama* is the first of the eight limbs of Yoga (meaning 'non-injury' and 'self-restraint'). Yogis represent the chakras in the spine as geometrical drawings. Tantrics use varied geometric patterns to represent deities or the many different aspects of life and as aids in meditation. Like the yantra, the egg-shaped *brahmanda*, the globe-shaped *saligrama* and the *shivalinga*, found mostly in stone and used for ritual, manifest a realization of the wholeness of the universe with its all-pervading subtle aspect.

Every deity in the Hindu religion has a *yantra* and a special mantra. *Yantra* is a symbolic way of worshipping a deity with a known form, while also recognizing the formless aspect. The presence of the deity is invoked through prayer and chanting of a mantra in an oral tradition handed down directly by the guru. This is part of the *diksha* or *upadesha* (instruction or initiation), which the guru transmits to the disciple.

Mantras are holy words used in spiritual practice according to the directions of the guru. Etymologically, *man-tra* comes from the word *manana,* which means 'reflection' or 'contemplation,' and *tra,* which signifies 'liberation' or 'protection.' Mantra has, therefore, two separate interpretations. It protects the seeker by deflecting difficulties and also operates as a form of contemplation and concentration, which grant liberation. Mantras date far back in time to the very origin of the Vedas. Every stanza in the Upanishads is also known as a mantra. Mantras are known as *vaidika* (if the source is Veda), or *tantrika* (if the source is Tantra). *Mantra Vidya* is the science that teaches how and at which time to use a mantra. *Vaidika mantras* have restrictions concerning who, what, where, and when, whereas tantric mantras are generally short and simple, without any strict specifications. This weighs in the favor of tantric mantras, making them more universally accepted and applicable.

Tantric mantras are full of *vijaksharas* or 'root and seed' mantras, making them extremely powerful. They are not prayers but rather a mystical formula combining different letters or a single syllable full of deep spiritual significance. It is called *nadabrahma*, a sound symbol embodying form or formless with tremendous power to arouse consciousness in a person.

On the deeper metaphysical level the body or tool becomes *yantra*, the senses are *tantra* and living in God-consciousness is mantra. A life of discipline immersed in God, becomes inner Tantra.

Tantra as a Philosophy

Tantra traces its roots back to the Vedas, and through the ages it has evolved into a simplified and popular form of Vedic philosophy. Tantra is a synthesis of Vedanta, Samkhya, Purvamimamsa, and Yoga.

Samkhya introduces the concepts of *prakriti* and *purusha*; *prakriti* being the inert nature or material cause, and *purusha* the efficient cause. *Maya,* in the Vedanta, is portrayed in the Shvetashvatara Upanishad (4:10) as *anirvachaniya,* an entity 'without any description' or without beginning, nescient, inexplicable, and illusory.

In Vedanta, it is essential to be free from the illusive power of *maya* to be in truth, whereas in Tantra, *maya* (in the form of *shakti*) is accepted as a sacred principle necessary to experience reality and truth. In reality *prakriti, maya,* and *shakti* are the same.

In Tantra, *shakti* is also known as *mahamaya* or *prakriti maya* and it is portrayed as the dynamic aspect through which it is possible to achieve the supreme state of realization. *Shakti* is translated as energy and strength. The Upanishads instruct that a person with strength can reach the supreme goal; therefore, tantrics concentrate on the worship of *shakti*, the supreme energy.

In Samkhya, the ultimate reality is the *purusha*, which is essentially the real cause of all activity. The Vedanta explains this in the following way:

ekam eva advitīyam brahma
"Brahman is the one without a second."

Brahman is portrayed here as outstanding in his singleness. He stands far and alone. In contrast, Tantra uses the name of Shiva as *paramashiva* (Supreme Shiva). Samkhya gives us the example of *purusha* and *prakriti,* Vedanta mentions Brahman and *maya,* and Tantra describes the play of Shiva and Shakti, different ways of describing the same phenomenon.

The relationship between Shiva and Shakti is like fuel and fire; water and its cooling nature; potential and kinetic energy; a word and its meaning. They are at once one, and one in two. Each one is such an integral part of the other, that they are completely inseparable. The inactive state is Shiva, and when it becomes active, it turns into Shakti. Shiva is formless, but Shakti has a form. In some tantric texts as well as in the Puranas, Shiva is described symbolically as *ardhanarishvara*, half male and half female, one being with two manifestations.

According to tantric philosophy, God had no attributes before creation *(nirguna parameshvara)* and *shakti* remained latent and inherent. When *shakti* was awakened from the dormant stage, God acquired attributes (*saguna*). Thus, the first state in the process of creation is *shakti.* From *shakti* emanated *paranada,* the un-manifested sound or vibration, and the sound generated *parabindu,* or the upper point. From the highest point stemmed *aparabindu,* or the lower point, which is identified as The Shiva Principle. After this stage came *bija* (the seed), source of the twenty-four cosmic principles. From the seed sprung *aparanada,* or the lower sound or vibration, which is considered the union of Shiva and Shakti. *Aparabindu,* or lower point, is none other than Shiva himself, from whom the five principal deities emerge: Sadashiva, Vishnu, Brahma, Ishana, and Rudra. (*SeeTable 4, page 50.*)

Creation of life was divided into four types. From the first stage arose all the organisms that grew out of sweat and moisture. Plants that germinated from seeds were the second stage. Animals that sprouted from eggs comprised the third stage and last of all came the animals, including humans, who are born from a fetus. The same universal soul is present in all, but each individual soul is known as *jiva*. In reality, every *jiva* is in truth Shiva, but because of ignorance, we are unable to experience our divine nature and merge in universal awareness. Through the practice of self-discipline, meditation, *japa, puja*, and allied rituals, the mind is cleansed and becomes free from such limitations. When a spiritual seeker is able to fully comprehend one's latent spirituality, *jiva* becomes Shiva.

Tantric texts, as well as the Vedanta and yogic literature all coincide in the description that the three bodies (gross, astral, and causal), making up every individual, are in reality just like three separate layers of clothes concealing the luminous soul.

The gross body stems from the five elements; earth, water, fire, air, and space, and will — after its demise — disintegrate back to these same elements. Since the gross body is physical and tangible in nature, it is subject to the perception of the five sense organs: sight, sound, touch, taste, and smell. The gross body has limited capabilities and it is finite in essence.

The astral body is psychological in nature and the mind — with its components of memory, thoughts, ego, and emotions — plays a dominant role. The astral body consists of nineteen limbs; the five organs of action, the five organs of perception, the five *pranas* or vital breaths, and the four inner instruments (the mind, intellect, ego, and memory). Since the astral body is subtle and moves in the realm of feelings and imagination, the area of its activities is quite broad.

The causal body is the last wrapping of the embodied soul. It is the cause of bondage, but carries within it the seed of liberation. Due to ignorance, human beings are condemned to a recurrent cycle of birth-death-rebirth, but once seekers become empowered to lift the veil and discover the unity of the universal soul, they experience the joy of liberation. At this point all three bodies dissolve, becoming one with the Absolute.

In tantric texts, these three bodies are described as *om tat sat.* The gross body is *om,* represented in the five lower chakras. (*See Table 1, page* 48.) The astral body is *tat,* travelling between the center of knowledge (*vishuddha chakra*) and the soul center (*ajna chakra*). The causal body is *sat,* and can only be felt while immersed in the *sahasrara chakra,* or the abode of God inside the cranium just below the crown of the head.

The Seven Steps

Tantric texts are vast, complex, and extremely elaborate, creating differences in both understanding and practice. There are seven modes of practice (*achara*) related to *sadhana*, which represent the seven steps in order to progress in the spiritual path. Each step must be integrated into daily life and coupled with belief, faith (*vishvasa*), and devotion to God, in order to reach the goal. (*See Table 2, page 49*)

The first step is *Vedachara,* or Vedic practice. The Vedas are considered the source of knowledge and philosophical principles, and since the tantric tradition is grounded in the Vedas, a tantric's life is based on Vedantic teachings. The scriptures promulgate that a daily routine must be implanted in a disciplined way. As a first step, a spiritual seeker should wake up every morning at dawn, perform inward and outward cleansing, chant some specific mantras according to the prescribed manner, follow a regulated diet, and practice moderation in sexual activities. This strict mode of conduct is designed to prepare a devotee for the rigors of spiritual life.

The second step, *Vaishnavachara* or *Vaishnavite* practice, is centered on Lord Vishnu. At this stage spiritual vows have to be taken which include: no conjugal life, no violence or cruelty, no blame or accusation, no falsehood, no ritualistic practices at night. Devotees try to immerse their whole life in divinity with the profound understanding that the entire creation is none other than a manifestation of Lord Vishnu.

In the third step, *Shaivachara* or *Shaivite* practice, Lord Shiva is considered the presiding deity. By meditating on Shakti, the divine state of Shiva is experienced since Shiva and Shakti are one and the same. Behind every work, the seeker is conscious that Shiva is the real doer. There must be no trace of cruelty, even to animals. Since Lord Shiva is considered to have his abode in the cremation grounds, tantric rituals are practiced there. This form of devotion cultivates the perception of Shiva as the indwelling Self.

The fourth step, *Dakshinachara*, is known as the practice with the right hand or favorable path. In this mode of worship, the seeker must perform all rituals with the right hand. The presiding deity is Dakshinakali, whose right foot, significantly, is slightly forward as she stands on Shiva's chest. Practitioners of this path follow prescribed modes of *sadhana* and the *varnashrama* system, based on castes and the four stages of life. It is essential to have faith, devotion, perception of inner energies, and a focused attention on *sat cit ananda Brahma,* since Brahman is the 'source of reality, consciousness, and absolute bliss.'

The fifth step, *Vamachara,* is the left-handed path involving *vama* or woman. It is sometimes called the unfavourable path, but this needs to be understood properly. In this *sadhana,* tantrics worship Kali, the Mother Divine, whose left foot is placed slightly in front as she stands on Shiva's chest. The seeker, therefore, uses the left hand in all ritualistic practices. It has been called 'unfavourable' because through this mode of practice negative propensities can be overcome very quickly. While ordinary people follow the way of pleasure and enjoyment, considering this to be favourable; a true spiritual seeker does the opposite and follows a seemingly unfavourable or difficult path, which involves renunciation and detachment, but is, however, rewarding in the end.

Many tantric practitioners consider themselves as *bhairava* or attendants of Shiva, and keep a *bhairavi* or female practitioner as a co-seeker. Within family life a wife can also participate in this mode of practice. In this way, a couple with purity of mind, expressed in thoughts, words, and deeds, will progress together in the spiritual field. The path of *Vamachara* is also known as *Chinachara*. Sage Vasistha is believed to have introduced it after his travels in Indonesia, Tibet, and China. In the course of time, many Buddhists and Tibetans practiced this path in order to reach liberation.

The sixth step, *Siddhantachara,* is the path of contemplation and meditation. *Siddhanta* means 'truth,' 'concepts,' and 'conclusion.' The spiritual seeker is no longer involved in external rituals, time and energy are instead devoted to inner contemplation and growth. Mental practice and discipline are the means to obtain realization.

The seventh and last step is known as *Kaulachara* or practice according to the *Kaulas*. Another name is *Kaula Marga* or the path of the *Kaulas*. The metaphorical interpretation of *kula* is a combination between *ku* 'the earth' or *brahmashakti* (manifested power of God) and *la*, which represents 'the seed' or *bija*. *Kula* is equivalent to *shakti* and through worship of the Divine Mother, source of all energy, supernatural experiences, and liberation are attained. In this practice, attention is focused on the *kundalini shakti,* also called *kula kundalini*.

Lord Shiva is known as *akula*. The joining of *kula kundalini* with *akula* is the union of Shiva and Shakti in the thousand-petal lotus located in the crown of the head. Such a feat is only accomplished through rigorous spiritual discipline, as energy must be channeled upwards to reach the source of life, *akula* becoming the ultimate attainment. In other words, through the practice of self-discipline and meditation, the dormant energy is manifested in the nine aspects of life. Otherwise known as *navakula*, these are:

Jiva tattva the principle of the individual soul,

Prakriti tattva the principle of nature, containing twenty-four aspects,

Dik the principle of ten directions, such as north, south, east, and west; the four corners north-east, north-west, south-east, south-west; above and below,

Kala the principle of time, both in relative and absolute terms,

Kshiti the earth element in the body, which regulates our relationship with the material world (the earth element is in the *muladhara chakra*),

Apa the principle of water (the water element is in the *svadhisthana chakra*),

Teja the principle of fire, represented by energy or strength (the fire element is in the *manipura chakra*),

Vayu the principle of air represented by the breath or *prana* (the air element is in the *anahata chakra*),

Akasha or the principle of space, outside and inside, experienced in meditation (the space element is in the *vishuddha chakra*).

The Triple Qualities of Nature

Spiritual life is an evolutionary process from animality to rationality and ultimately to the state of divinity. Each individual is potentially divine, but our divine qualities often remain unmanifested. Spiritual evolution arouses the latent divinity that lies dormant within us in order to reach a state of perfection. According to Vedanta, creation (*maya*) is pervaded by three governing qualities. By their permutation and combination an infinite variety of names, forms, and qualities are created. These aspects are also operating within each individual and make that person distinct from all others. Every individual has a predominant nature operating at any given time. These triple qualities of nature are:

tamas guna	(inert/dull), characterized by laziness and a constant need for sleep,
rajas guna	(aggressive/ambitious), identified by activity and enthusiasm,
sattva guna	(calm/spiritual), full of peace, happiness, and universal love.

The journey of a seeker is like climbing a ladder, and each, according to one's intent and qualities is assessed to have reached a specific rung. Significant are the qualities and attitudes, *bhavas*, of the seeker in determining each level. Tantric literature emphasizes three major *bhavas*:

Pashu bhava	animalistic behaviour determined by instincts and emotion,
Vira bhava	heroic behaviour portrayed as awareness in the midst of struggle, manifested in persistent effort,
Divya bhava	divinity, manifested in supreme love for all creation; an attitude of peace, bliss, and joy.

At the *pashu bhava* stage tantric seekers tend to follow ritualistic practices in a literal way. The *tamasic* quality in their nature is usually predominant. They practice rituals in order to gain temporary pleasures and occult powers such as *vashikarana,* or mental control over others; *marana,* or the ability to create trouble for others; *mohana,* or hypnotic power, and so on. These powers come almost automatically when the capacity to concentrate and control the mind has been perfected, but they should not be sought after or used because they block the way to liberation. Tantrics that become absorbed in physical pleasure, material gain, and worldly power are chained to the lowest level. A *pashu bhava* seeker dwells in one's animal nature, which is full of unsublimated passions of the lowest order.

The *vira bhava* stage is more evolved since the *rajasic* mind is more purified than the *tamasic* mind. At this point tantric seekers use symbolic practices in order to grow spiritually. The *rajasic* quality in their nature plays a major role due to an active inner struggle for improvement. The *rajasic* mind tries to cultivate virtues, and this implies enormous self-effort. *Rajasic* people are focused on the psychological and 'astral' aspects of their nature and interested in supernatural powers of a higher order such as *anima, mahima, laghuma,* or the art of experiencing oneself as very small or unusually large, extremely light or terribly heavy. Some *rajasic* people evolve and grow to become effortlessly established in the divine state of *divya bhava.*

The *divya bhava* stage is the highest form of tantric practice. There are no external manifestations or futile attempts to gain occult powers. Pivoted on the *sattvic,* such tantrics focus on mental worship in a state of deep meditation. They try to go beyond birth and death, and merge in the path of supreme love. *Pashu bhava, vira bhava,* and *divya bhava* can be compared with a bud, a flower, and a fruit evolving through a natural process to reach the highest state of realization; wherein there is no longer any regard for minor aspects such as pleasure or prosperity. Tantric practice leads to the experience and manifestation of divinity already present within us. (*See Table 2, page* 49.)

The Five Principles

Panchatattvas (the five principles) or *panchamakara* (the five words) beginning with the syllable *ma* represent the most misunderstood aspect within Tantra. In this mode of practice, the seeker uses five objects that start with the letter *m* in order to perform certain rituals:

Madya	wine/alcohol,
Mamsa	flesh/meat,
Matsya	fish,
Mudra	roasted or fried food,
Maithuna	coition.

According to some tantric practices these five elements are considered essential components. Unfortunately these words have been given a literal translation associating them with pleasure and enjoyment, and as such, have done great damage to Tantra as a spiritual science. The actual spiritual and metaphorical meaning is completely different, and has great relevance for a spiritual seeker. (*See Table 3, page* 49) For this potential misconception, it is insisted in tantric literature that the practice should only be performed under the strict supervision of a competent guru, or it will lead to extreme confusion or misapplication. When the five *tattvas* are applied literally by *sadhakas* immersed in the *pashu bhava* stage, the entire tantric system is demeaned and debased.

The *panchatattvas* or *panchamakara* are designed to promote spiritual evolution from one stage to another, eventually reaching a highly focused stage of single-mindedness. (*See Table 4, page* 50) The five principles are described in the following texts:

madyaṃ māmsaṃ tataḥ matsyo mudrā maithunaṃ eva ca
pancatattvamidaṃ devi nirvaṇa muktihetavah
makāra pancakaṃ devi devānāṃ api durlabham

(Gupta Sadhana Tantra)

"O Divine Lady! The *panchatattvas* (five principles) like wine, flesh, fish, fried cereals, and coition are required for liberation, which is not easily available, even to celestials."

nārcayet kālikāṃ deviṃ śāmbhavī sukha mokṣadām
madyaṃ māmsaṃ tatha matsayaṃ mudrāṃ ca maithunaṃ vinā
bāhmaṇo vīra bhāvena kalikāyai nivedayet

"Never worship Kali, the bestower of *shambhavi* (state of perfect meditation), happiness and liberation, without wine, flesh, fish, fire, and coition. The Brahmin with a heroic nature should offer these to Kalika."

madyai māmsaistathā matsyair mudrābhirmaithunairapi
stribhi sārdha mahāsāhuḥ arccayed jagadambikām
anyathā ca mahānindā gīyate panditaiḥ suraih
kāyena manasā vācā tasmāt tattva paro bhavet

"He is a great sage, who worships Jagadambika (Mother of the Universe) with wine, flesh, fish, fried food, and coition. Otherwise the scholars and priests will blame him. Through such worship he goes beyond body, mind, and speech. Therefore go beyond the *tattvas*."

A state of confusion and malpractice has arisen due to the misinterpretation of this kind of citations. The actual spiritual and metaphorical meaning is completely different, and has great relevance for a spiritual seeker. Through the direct guidance of a highly evolved guru and by the practice of deep meditation, the real hidden meaning of these texts can be expounded. To counteract this negative influence, other tantric sources have attempted to condemn these abuses by trying to restore purity within the system.

1) *Madya* (wine/alcohol):

In Sanskrit, *madya* has synonyms like *madhu, madira, soma,* and *sura*, which can mean 'wine,' but are also used to represent 'milk,' 'molasses,' and 'honey' (*madhutraya* or three types of *madhu*). The literal translation is, of course, 'intoxicating drink' or 'liquor,' but that is only a symbol for the subtler meaning. It is impossible to fully grasp spiritual reality without the guidance of a guru and the practice of deep meditation. Without these, ego tends to play a pivotal role, leading to scant and false interpretations. The following verse is an example:

pītvā pītvā punaḥ pitvā yāvad patati bhūtale
utthāya ca punaḥ pītvā punarjanma na vidyate

"Drink and drink (again and again) until you fall down (unconscious). Rise up and drink again, only then will you get liberation."

This kind of citation, if interpreted lightly, can be an aberration and taken by libertines to be an encouragement to delve in all kinds of vices under the guise of spirituality. Therefore the Kularnava Tantra quotes,

madya pānena manujo yadi siddhim labhavte vai
madya panaratāḥ sarve siddhiṃ gacchantu pāmarāḥ

"If through drinking alcohol a person will attain perfection, then all evil-minded alcoholics can attain it."

In the Agama Sara, a classical tantric textbook, the practice of drinking and intoxication is properly interpreted,

somadhāra kṣaret yātu brahmarandhrāt varānane
pītvānanda mayastān yeḥ sa eva madya sādhaka

"The flow of nectar, which comes from the aperture of the divine *brahmarandhra,* situated in the core of the thousand-petal lotus, once swallowed will give the blissful state of divine intoxication."

This is the real meaning of the wine that Lord Shiva speaks about in Tantra, and it blends well with his teachings and practice on the subject of Yoga. In the yogic exercise of *khechari mudra,* the tongue is pointed towards the fontanel, touching the uvula and even further, past the back of the palate. This practice results in a special secretion of saliva, which gives a soothing effect to the body and the mind in a feeling of divine intoxication. This type of saliva is known as the 'wine of the yogis' and is considered the gateway to enter the state of deep meditation.

In the Bible it is said that Jesus was often falsely accused of being a glutton and a drunkard because he seemed to be in a strange sort of state that was similar to intoxication. Sometimes, when his disciples offered him food he would say, "I have already eaten." To counteract their surprise he would add, "You do not know the nature of the food and drink I live on." Those that did not know Lord Jesus well and were given over to doubts, spread rumors that he was overpowered by alcohol, but such intoxication was none other than the result of deep meditation and an endless communion with God.

The Kaivalya Tantra, a renowned tantric scripture says,

yaduktaṃ parama brahma nirvikāraṃ nirnjanam
tasmin pramadana jñānaṃ tanmadyaṃ parikīrtitam

"Being completely absorbed in *parambrahman*, which is described as (a state) free from all modification and description, gives a divine intoxication known as wine."

Deep contact and communion with God is intoxicating and becomes possible through Yoga and meditation. Just like an alcoholic cannot survive without alcoholic beverages, a truly spiritual person considers meditation to be an essential part of life. In tantric rituals a substitute can be used, known as *anukalpa*. Tender coconut water in copper pots is the *anukalpa* for wine during ritualistic practice.

2) *Mamsa* (flesh/meat):

The second practice is known as *mamsa sadhana* and it is related to the consumption of flesh or meat. As in the previous example, if a text is interpreted in accordance to the primary meaning, it can be grossly misconstrued. When these steps are followed literally, without understanding their true import, it is impossible to become released from the clutch of the senses. In tantric texts there is the following description,

māmsa tu trividhā proktaṃ jala bhūcara khecara
yasmāt kasmāt samānitaṃ yena kena vighātitam
tat sarvaṃ devatāprītaiḥ bhavet eva na samsayāh

"There are three types of flesh, know it clearly, from the creatures of the land, water, and air. These can be caught by any means and killed in any manner, and offered to the gods. This will please them without any doubt."

Though it is true that in the name of many religions, numerous animals have been offered and sacrificed at the altar of God, the great prophets and masters have always opposed and attempted to reform this cruel ritual. God is manifested and present throughout creation. How could God be pleased with the destruction and slaying of animals?

The Yoga Upadesha says,

jupaṃ kṛtvā paśuṃ kṛtvā kṛtvā rudhira kardamam
yadyeva gaṁyate svargaṃ narakaṃ kena gamyate

"If by preparing the altar of sacrifice and butchering animals, soaking the soil with blood, if such carnivorous people will go to heaven, then who will go to hell?"

The Kularnava Tantra warns,

māmsa bhakṣaṇa mātreṇa yadi puṇyagatir bhavet
loke māmsasinaḥ sarve puṇya bhājo bhavantunah

"If by eating flesh, people attain merits and virtues in this world, let the entire flesh-eaters get liberation."

The real metaphorical meaning of *mamsa* or flesh is described in the same text,

māngalya jananāt devi satcidānanda dānatah
sarvadeva priyattvāt ca māmsa iti abhidhīyate

"That which gives rise to auspiciousness and bestows eternal consciousness and bliss, that which pleases all the gods, is known as flesh."

The word *mamsa* is composed of two parts, *mam* and *sa,* which represent two divine attainments — *mangalya* (auspiciousness) and *sat-cit-ananda* (eternity, consciousness, and bliss). *Mamsa* is a state of spiritual enlightenment that brings eternal, auspicious bliss.

Lord Shiva explains the means to attain this blissful state,

mā śabdat rasanā jñeyā taddamśanāt rasanā priye
sadā yo bhakṣayet devi sa eva māmsa sādhakāh

"Know that *ma* represents 'the tongue,' and whoever constantly devours it, O Devi, is truly a *mamsa sadhaka* (practitioner of eating flesh)."

To eat one's tongue, or swallow it temporarily, is the yogic technique known as *khechari mudra.* In the Hatha Yoga Pradipika of Svatmarama Yogindra, the practice of *khechari mudra* is described as eating beef and drinking wine,

gomāmsa bhakṣayet nityam pibet amarā vāruṇim
tamahaṃ kulīna manye itare kulaghātakāh

"Those who eat *gomamsa* (flesh of a cow) and drink *varuni* (strong liquor), I consider them highly cultivated people, others are contemptible."

At first glance it would appear that Lord Shiva is urging devotees to devour beef and consume alcohol, but the subsequent verse offers the hidden meaning,

go śabde noditā jihvā tat praveśa hi talusca
go māmsa bhakṣaṇaṃ iti mahā pātaka nāśanam

"The word *go* connotes the tongue. When one swallows it, this signifies the eating of *go-mamsa* (the flesh of the tongue) or beef. Such practice destroys all evil in a person."

Devotees immersed in this discipline are truly practicing *mamsa sadhana.* The Kularnava Tantra has an additional interpretation related to the slaughter of animals and eating of flesh,

pāpa puṇya paśuṃ hatvā jnāna khadgena yogavit
pare layaṃ nayet cittaṃ palāśīti nigadyate

"A yogi, with the sword of knowledge, can slaughter the two beasts of virtues and vices. The mind of such a person rests on the Supreme and he is known as a flesh-eater."

People are confined in equal measure by their attachment to virtue or to vice. While vice breeds disease and suffering, virtue offers temporary glory and limited enjoyment. Both are the cause of bondage. If vice can be portrayed as a binding with a heavy rusty iron chain, virtue binds us equally with an elaborate gold ornament. Meditation severs the bonds that keep human beings bound to the cycle of birth-death-rebirth; pleasure and pain; good and evil. By destroying the attachment to both virtue and vice with the sword of Self-knowledge, a yogi becomes a true flesh eater, constantly absorbed in God through deep meditation. In this manner, the inner animals such as anger, pride, ignorance, attachment, ego, and jealousy, which plague the soul, are slain or destroyed.

Mamsa can also be split into two root words: *ma* and *amsa* — *ma* represents 'the tongue' and *amsa* is that which is 'born from (the tongue),' i.e., 'taste' and 'speech.' An additional meaning of *mamsa sadhana* is to control food intake by occasional fasting (taste) and to discipline life through the deliberate practice of silence (speech). The *anukalpa,* or symbolic substitute in rituals, for flesh is salt, white sesame seeds, or garlic and onion.

3) *Matsya* (fish):

The third principle or *tattva* is *matsya* or fish. The less developed type of seekers, still imbued in the animalistic *pashu bhava* stage, take this concept to heart and offer three types of fish to the Divine Mother, their presiding deity. The fish can be raw, deep-fried, or roasted; with or without bones; from the pond, the river, or the sea. It is offered in worship and later on eaten as *prasad* or consecrated food. Sweet-water fish is preferred to seafood. The *anukalpa* is white eggplant, red radish, red spinach, red lentils, and roasted vegetables. The metaphorical interpretation of *matsya* involves inner transformation.

The Kularnava Tantra says,

māyā malādi śamanāt mokṣamārga nirūpaṇāt
aṣṭaduhkhādi virahāt matsyeti parikīrtitah

"*Matsya* (fish) is that which removes the impurities of delusion from life, shows clearly the path of liberation, and makes one free from the eight types of suffering (being in the womb, birth, marriage, worldly life, mental anguish, disease, old age, and death)."

The Kailash Tantra instructs,

gangā yamunāyormadhye dvau matsyaṃ carataḥ sadā
tau matsyau bhakṣayet yastu sa bhavet matsya sādhakah

"In the rivers Ganga and Yamuna, two fish always roam. One who devours these two fish becomes a *matsya sadhaka* (fish worshipper)."

The rivers Ganga and Yamuna represent the two spinal channels in the body called the *ida* and the *pingala,* which begin in the base of the spine and end in the left and right nostrils respectively. The inhalation and exhalation of the breath is allegorically described as the coming and going of two fish. The seeker who 'consumes' these two fish by the practice of breath-control, will gain inner tranquility and attain the state of liberation.

The Kularnava Tantra explains this in the following verse,

matsamāna sarva bhūte sukha duhkhamidaṃ priye
iti yat sāttvika jnānaṃ tan matsya parikīrtitam

"To offer fish in worship means to perceive Me (Shiva) equally in all, and accept the duality of life like pleasure and pain with equanimity, by being established in pure knowledge (*sattvika-jñana*)."

The same scripture goes on to elaborate,

manasādindriya grāmaṃ samyamyātmani yojayet
matsyāsi sa bhavet devi itare prāṇi ghātakāh

"One who disciplines the mind and the senses and unites them with the Self, is a true eater of fish. O Devi! The others are simply killing the living animals (*prani,* here refers to fish)."

Matsya teaches the spiritual seeker to eliminate all restlessness and achieve inner tranquility, purity, and peace through breath-control and by remaining established in a state of pure knowledge, experiencing the presence of God everywhere.

4) *Mudra* (parched grain):

The fourth *tattva* or principle in Tantra is *mudra.* In Sanskrit, the word *mudra* has multiple meanings; 'seal,' 'stamp,' 'coin,' 'passport,' 'image,' 'parched grain,' 'the position of the fingers,' 'a yogic exercise,' and 'the art of making love.' In tantric practices *mudra* is used in three different ways:

i) Fried food/parched grain:
Parched grain is offered in a ritual to the Divine Mother. There are three types of grain. A special white rice, barley, or wheat fried in ghee, is considered the best kind of offering. A slightly lesser grade is puffed rice and other sweetened cereals. Finally, the darker type of grain is also acceptable but considered of lower quality.

ii) Hand gesture or position of the fingers:
In Hindu rituals (including classical dance), specific hand gestures are used symbolically, to invoke, to welcome, to please, to offer, and so on. Within the tantric scriptures there is a description of nine *mudras* considered to be pleasing to the Divine Mother, which include: *pasa* or noose, *ankuhsa* or hook, *vara* or blessing, *abhaya* or assurance, *khadga* or sword, *charma* or shield, *damaru,* tabor, or small drum, *shara* or arrow, and *musala* or mace.

iii) *Mudra* is interpreted as the art of making love or as a yogic exercise:
In classical yogic literature there is a detailed description of different forms of *asanas* or postures, which if used effectively and combined with a breathing technique bring about exceptional self-control and pave the way to enter a deep state of meditation. In the Gheranda Samhita, as taught by Sage Gheranda, a description is made of twenty *mudras*. A few examples are: *mahamudra, yonimudra, sambhavi mudra, shakti chalini mudra,* and *ashvini mudra.* These *mudras* help the seeker to gain mastery over the body, mind, and breath in order to progress on the spiritual path. It is important to remember that all these *mudras* must be practiced under the direct guidance and supervision of an advanced practitioner.

The Agama Sara, a well-known tantric text, describes the inner meaning of *mudra,*

sahasrāre mahāpadme karnikā mudritascaret
ātma tatraiva devesi kevala paradopamah

sūryokoti pratikaśaḥ candra koti suśītalah
atīva kamaniyasca mahakunḍalinī yutah
yasya jñānodayāstatra mudra sādhaka ucyate

"O Divine! In the crown of the head, in the center of the thousand-petal lotus, there is the presence of the soul, as clear as mercury. Although, it is brilliant like millions of suns, it is still cool and soothing like millions of moons. It is also equally beautiful. One, who realizes this by being united with *kundalini*, is truly a practitioner of *mudra*. Such a seeker has gained the state of wisdom and is known as *mudra sadhaka* (seeker achieving perfection in *mudra*)."

Mudra has also been interpreted as a kind of renunciation,

satsangena bhavet muktiḥ asatsangena bandhanam
asatsanga mudrāṇaṃ yat tanmudrā parikīrtitam

"Good company is the cause of liberation whereas bad company brings bondage. The art of renouncing bad company is known as *mudra*."

During the practice of meditation, various coin-shaped colours can be experienced. This is described as *mudra* or 'coin-in-meditation.' Etymologically, *mudra* is divided into three parts: *mud* means 'pleasure,' *drav* is 'to melt,' *ra* is 'to give.' *Mudra* can be interpreted as that which pleases God, makes the heart melt, and frees us from all vices by giving the joy of fulfillment. In both meditation and ritualistic worship, many types of *mudras* can be used. Only through spiritual discipline can a sincere seeker evolve on the path of enlightenment.

5) *Maithuna* (coition):

The incorporation of sexuality in worship and spiritual practice has brought about a great deal of misunderstanding. The depiction of Shiva and Parvati as a symbol of cosmic union has led many so-called practitioners of Tantra to live with partners, experimenting in sexual techniques under the guise of spirituality. This sexual approach has debased Tantra from a pure, spiritual science to an amalgamation of contradictory principles, adulterated between the search for God and the search for pleasure. In the tantric scriptures it is described,

maithunaṃ parama tattvaṃ sṛṣtisthityanta kāraṇam
maithunāt jāyate siddhi brahmajñānaṃ sudurlabham

"*Maithunam* (conjugation) is the supreme principle, the cause of creation, sustenance, and dissolution. Through *maithuna*, one achieves perfection and gains the extremely rare knowledge of the Absolute."

Another tantric text claims,

kulakuṇḍalinī śakti dehināṃ dehadhāriṇi
taya śivasya samyogaḥ maithunaṃ parikīrtitam

"The power of *kundalini* remains in the body. When it is united with Shiva it is known as *maithuna* or coition."

The Kularnava Tantra, however, denounces the literal approach to *maithuna* (sexual intercourse) in spiritual practice stating,

strī sambhogena devesi yadi mokṣaṃ labhate vai
sarvepi jantavo loke muktāḥ syu strī niṣevanāt

"If by enjoyment of women, O Divine, people would attain liberation, then all the animals would be liberated as they live the life of copulation."

The same source asserts,

para shaktyatma mithuna samyogānanda īśvarah
muktāste maithunaṃ tat syāt itare strīnisevakāh

"The ones who through self-discipline and meditation can unite *parashakti* (the cosmic energy hidden in the body) with the inner

Self, experience the perennial source of bliss and realize God. They are truly free and liberated through such conjugation, and the others are only slaves of women."

The real sexual intercourse is between the female body-nature and male soul or God-nature, through every breath. The yogic state presupposes the realization of this ceaseless union of body and soul. This realization can only be attained through *sadhana* involving breath regulation and self-control. In ritualistic worship, offering some flowers like *aparajita* or *agasti* (special flowers used in worship) through *yonimudra* and *kurmamudra* (special hand gestures) is the *anukalpa* for *maithuna.* In yogic practice Shiva or the invisible soul is always in coition with the body and maintaining its life through inhalation; union with God in every breath is the real act of perennial love.

Table One Classification of Chakras

NAME	REGION	PETALS	ELEMENTS	VIJAKSHARA	MATRIKA	COLOUR
Muladhara	coccyx region	4	earth	lam	va, sha, sa	golden yellow
Svadhisthana	sacral region	6	water	vam	ba, bha, ma,ya, ra,la	colourless
Manipura	lumbar region	10	fire	ram	da, dha, na, ta, tha, da, dha, pa, pha	red
Anahata	dorsal region	12	air	yam	ka, kha, ga, gha, na, ca, cha, ja, jha, na, pa, pha	smoky
Vishuddha	cervical region	16	ether	sham	all sixteen vowels	smoky white
Ajna	pituitary region	2	beyond elements (mahat)	ham kshma	ham, ksha	smoky white
Sahasrara	fontanel	1,000			om	colourless

Table Two Classification of *Acharas* (modes of conduct) *Ashramas* (stages of life), and *Gunas* (the predominant qualities)

QUALITIES	BHAVA	ACARA/ PRACTICE	STATE OF LIVING	SPIRITUAL EVOLUTION	MODE OF SUFFERING
tamasic	pashu	vedacara	brahmacarya celibacy	beginners	adhibhautika (physical)
tamasic and rajasic	vira	siddhantacara dakshinacara vamacara	grihastha (family)	intermediate state	adhidaivika (mental)
rajasic and sattvic	vira and divya	kulacara	vanaprastha (retirement)	state of maturity	adhyatmika (unforeseen)
pure sattvic	divya	yogacara	sannyasa (complete renunciation)	realization	tapatrayatita (free from suffering)

Table Three Panchamakara (panchatattvas), the Five Principles Beginning with *Ma*

FIVE MA'S	TAMASIC (literal/ physical/gross)	RAJASIC (anukalpa/substitute)	SATTVIC (metaphorical/symbolic)
madya- wine/ alcohol	made of molasses/fruit juice or fermented cereals	milk in a brass pot; coconut water in a brass pot; honey in a brass pot	saliva through khechari mudra, attainment of extreme love for God
mamsa- flesh	animals of the sea, land, air	salt, garlic, onion, white sesame	keep tongue rolled up; acceptance of God as source of all auspiciousness
matsya-	large but few bones; no bones; small but many bones	white coloured eggplant, red coloured radish, red leaf vegetables	inner purity;freedom fish from maya; breath control; to see God in all
mudra- physical posture for enjoyment	fried food with ghee; white colour; puffed rice or fried cereals	position of the fingers during ritualistic practices	practice of different mudras during meditation; to eliminate all evils; to experience inner peace
maithuna- coition	physical union with partner	to offer special flowers like aparajita or agasti; with red sandal wood	to experience union of parashakti with the soul, kundalini with Shiva, to experience samadhi

Table Four The Five Principles Integrated

madya	Prana (exhalation)	Vishnu
mamsa	apana (inhalation)	Brahma
matsya	samana (harmonization)	Rudra
mudra	udana (evolution)	Ishvara
maithuna	vyana (perception of pervasion)	Sadasiva

Spiritual Significance of the Cremation Ground

The cremation ground plays an important role within the Hindu system. When a person dies, the body is burnt to ashes in a funeral pyre, and the five constituent elements — the earth, water, fire, air, and space — in the body return to their original source. Ordinary people consider the cremation ground as a place of sadness and desolation, but a sadhu regards it as sacred ground, the abode of Shiva and Kali, the symbols of changelessness. Metaphorically, Lord Shiva is the personification of knowledge, non-attachment, and liberation. In each human body, Lord Shiva is seated in the *sahasrara* or the crown of the head. A seeker becomes united with Shiva when — through the power of concentration — one retracts the outgoing energy or *shakti* from the lower chakras and concentrates explicitly on the *sahasrara*. This state is known as *jiva-shiva-milana* or the union between the *kundalini shakti* with *parama shiva*.

A strong presence of death pervades the cremation ground generating detachment and dispassion in a devotee who realizes the futility and transitoriness of life. Recognizing the enduring permanence of Shiva and Shakti, the practitioner experiences the inner meaning of life in the proximity of death. Such recognition of opposites on the cremation ground deepens one's meditation.

The most auspicious time for effective tantric rituals is the new moon at midnight. Lord Shiva and Mother Kali are worshipped on such special occasions with elaborate *panchamakara sadhana* or five *m* principles discussed above. Depending on the practitioner's tantric tradition and the level of understanding, various stipulated objects are offered. Extremist groups do not shy away from offering their own blood during rituals. Tantrics often practice their rituals in a group but at other times they sit in a circle (forming a chakra) and follow their own independent methodology.

In the dance of cosmic energy everything undergoes constant change except Shiva, or the Supreme Soul. He is by nature changeless. The world is nothing but a cremation place of the old and a cradle-place for the new, since that which undergoes change is bound to perish but will eventually be reborn in a new form. This change of outlook brings more detachment for the outer world and a deeper more enduring love within for the absolute and eternal.

Shava Sadhana

Shava Sadhana means 'corpse meditation,' and some tantrics take this practice literally. Living in the cremation ground, they use dead bodies for specific rituals. Such extreme practice is rejected in other traditions. A physical posture in Hatha Yoga known as *shava asana* or the inert posture constitutes a complete relaxation technique that brings about rejuvenation and freedom from stress and strain.

In the Isha Upanishad, this process is taken a step further in a mantra, *bhashmantam shariram* or 'consider your body as having been burnt into ashes.' During deep meditation, a spiritual seeker goes beyond body consciousness to experience a state of inner awakening known as *so'ham,* 'I am That' (the Absolute), and dissolves into oneness with the whole of creation. A true practitioner is one who experiences the transitory nature of the body in its ultimate stage through meditation. The devotee ascends to the *sahasrara* (to the crown of the head) by withdrawing the *prana* or the energy principle from the base of the spine. Body consciousness is transformed into cosmic consciousness. When the gross body appears to be dead (breathless stage), it has reached the *samadhi* state. For both tantrics and yogis the practice is known as *shava sadḥana* or corpse meditation, and it is performed with the deep awareness that the body is lifeless, inert, without the presence of the soul.

Munda Sadhana

Munda Sadhana can be interpreted as finding an appropriate place for meditation. The scriptures abound with elaborate descriptions of suitable places for spiritual exercises. Suggestions include isolated and beautiful spots such as a temple, a riverbank, a mountain valley, a place close to a pond or lake, a well-ventilated cave, or a room that is quiet and clean.

In tantric texts there are two additional requirements. The first comes under the heading of *panchavati* or an assemblage of five special trees planted together, but opinions vary regarding the nature of the five holy trees. Traditional texts mention the following trees:

Ashoka	Jonisia Ashoka (a tree with red flowers),
Villva	Wood apple,
Bata	Banyan tree,
Dhatri (amalaka)	Emblic Myrrbalan,
Ashvattha	Peepal or the holy fig tree.

According to the *Gospel of Ramakrishna* the *neem* tree (*margosa)* is included instead of the *aṣhoka.*

More significant for the tantrics is the practice of *panchamundi asana.* The ideal place for meditation in this practice is to stand on the burial ground of the heads of five beings: a human, a snake, a monkey, a jackal, and a dog. The symbolic meaning of this ritual is to sit above the five lower centers, burying their restless qualities by remaining in the sixth center *(ajna chakra)* or the seventh center (*sahasrara chakra).* In this way, the sincere seeker is freed from dubious propensities since each animal skull corresponds to one of the five tendencies of the lower chakras. The dog, in the role of guardian to material prosperity, represents the *muladhara* or money center; the snake, embodiment of the need to copulate, coils up in the *svadhisthana* or sexual center; the jackal, always searching for food and prey is at the *manipura* or navel center; the restless monkey, filled with variable emotions, sits at the *anahata* or heart center; the human skull, expressing the constant search for intellectual, religious, and philosophical knowledge, finds its place in the *vishuddha chakra*.

The inner meaning of burying the five animal heads is to ascend progressively from the lower chakras until unity is reached with the Supreme Self, or *paramashiva,* in the *sahasrara* at the crown of the head. The only way to resist the delusive attraction of the lower chakras and find eternal bliss is by raising consciousness in this way.

Kapalika

It is a very common sight to find a tantric who keeps a human skull in his possession, especially the skull of a virgin, coloured with vermilion, and worshipped to invoke magical and supernatural powers. A human skull is also used as a food bowl for eating and drinking. But a truly spiritual life is never an external show; the dress, the rosary, the red-mark on the forehead are all meaningless unless the change in attitude is internalized and completely sincere, and one is always focused on inner transformation.

The word *Kapalika* comes from *kapala,* which means 'the head' or 'the crown of the head.' *Kapalika* metaphorically means to be established in the cranium with full concentration fixed in the *ajna* and *sahasrara chakras*. The place for spiritual evolution is the source of every thought and activity in the brain.

Aghora Sadhana

The word *aghora* is derived from the root word *ghora,* which means 'darkness' and 'fear.' *A-ghora,* therefore, stands for the contrary, 'illumination,' 'calmness,' and 'peace.' *Aghora sadhana* is a conscious effort to maintain mental equanimity. This is a state sought after by every sincere seeker.

There is a special group of tantrics that live in the cremation ground, following their own rituals without any visible discipline. They remain completely naked and smear their body with ashes collected from the funeral pyres. Since they live in the cremation ground, cut off from the world, it is believed that they consume human flesh. Their peculiar behaviour has fostered a profound dread about Tantra.

In a symbolic way, an *aghora sadhaka*, in his very nakedness, represents detachment from body consciousness. The consumption of human flesh can also be interpreted metaphorically, as a form of self-contentment. In the New Testament, Jesus said, "If you eat my flesh and drink my blood, then you will have your place in Heaven."

Darkness represents ignorance, whereas knowledge brings forth light. *Aghora* means to eliminate ignorance completely, without leaving any trace. As a devotee enters the state of deep meditation, one will gradually penetrate the veil of darkness *(ghora)* and experience Inner Light.

Guru and Disciple

Lord Shiva is the eternal guru and Parvati, his divine consort, is his faithful disciple (*sishya*). The dialogue between Shiva and Parvati teaches us an intricate spiritual truth. A worthy guru will impart sacred knowledge to a qualified student with the utmost love and care. A deserving disciple becomes the instrument to carry on the weight of such divine heritage, not only for the purpose of self-transformation but also for the more delicate role of future transmission. Since Tantra teaches a practical form of spirituality, it categorically underlines the need of a guru as a guide on the spiritual journey.

The Mahanirvana Tantra says,

bahu janmārijitaiḥ puṇyaiḥ sadguru yadi labhyate
tadā tat vaktrato labdhvā janma sāphalyaṃ āpnuyāt

"Due to the profound merits of a previous life, when one is fortunate to get a qualified guru, one is able to transform life and achieve success through his instruction."

The guru, through the example of self-discipline and spiritual attainment, can dispel the darkness of ignorance from the heart and the mind of a disciple.

In the Mahanirvana Tantra the following explanation is found,

mantradātā guruhproktaḥ mantrānāṃ parama guruh
parāpara gurutvaṃ hi parameṣṭhi gurustvaham

"One who initiates a disciple by giving a mantra is the guru. The mantra itself is the *parama guru* (superior guru), you (O Parvati) are *parapara guru* (supreme guru), and I (Shiva) am *paramesthi guru* (eternal guru)."

In the scriptures it is stated that a competent guru must be a person of pure parentage, descending from a Brahmin family and possessing great self-control. He should be familiar with the true meaning and real essence of the scriptures. He must be well acquainted with *puja* (worship), *homa* (the offering of oblations into the holy fire), *dhyana* (meditation), *japa* (the repetition of the divine name), and he should have thorough knowledge of Yoga. In addition, he must be full of love and have a peaceful disposition.

Tantra warns seekers of accepting false gurus, who exhibit outward erudition and holiness but are inwardly motivated by greed, hidden desires, and base instincts.

The *sishya* or disciple must also possess characteristics suitable to progress in spiritual life. The Vedantic texts prescribe that a worthy disciple must have the following attributes:

i) Discrimination,

ii) Freedom from desire for sense-enjoyment and accumulation of fame and fortune,

iii) The six-fold qualities such as control of the mind; control of the senses; fortitude; ability to withdraw the mind from external objects; faith; the power of concentration and awareness of the inner Self,

iv) A distinct longing for liberation.

A sincere seeker will progress in the spiritual path through love, devotion, truth, inner strength, and vigor. But a person who is habitually deceitful, earns money dishonestly, injures others, or cannot find a qualified guru, will not reach the highest goal.

The Guru's Role

bhūya eva mahābāho śṛṇu me paramam vacah
yat te ham priyamāṇāya vakṣyāmi hitakāmyayā

(Bhagavad Gita 10:1)

"O Mighty-armed Arjuna! Hear my words, which I impart to you who are dear to me, with a desire for your welfare."

The need for a guru is stressed in nearly all spiritual practices. Tantra emphasizes even more the need for a spiritual guide who can actively help the seeker to overcome the obstacles in life to achieve liberation.

It is extremely rare to find a guru who removes the suffering of disciples, helping them to evolve and to achieve supreme bliss. In the above verse, Lord Krishna is telling Arjuna, you are very dear to me because you are sincere and I am only concerned with your highest welfare, so please listen to me. The master wants the welfare and complete development of disciples. He wants them to excel in such a way that they may become greater than the master himself. Such is the unconditional love of the master for his students.

As described in tantric texts, a qualified guru should have the following qualities:

i) Tranquility and a peaceful countenance,

ii) Self-control over the mind and senses,

iii) Belonging to a pious family (in the scriptures specific allusion is made to the Brahmins),

iv) Humility devoid of all traces of ego and arrogance,

v) Dressed in sacred robes (ochre-coloured),

vi) Ingrained good habits; free from anger, vanity, and greed,

vii) Enjoying a good reputation; firmly established in spirituality,

viii) Transparent mind and activities,

ix) Diligent and efficient in spiritual practice,

x) Possessing wisdom; thorough knowledge of the essence of the Vedas, Agamas, and other related scriptures,

xi) Belonging to an *ashrama*; following the practical instructions of his own guru or lineage of masters,

xii) Having a meditative outlook, with thorough knowledge of Yoga,

xiii) Well-versed in Tantra and mantras,

xiv) A compassionate disciplinarian,

xv) Immersed in a permanent state of bliss.

The Disciple's Role

tad viddhi praṇipātena paripraśnena sevayā
upadekṣanti te jñānaṃ jñāninastattvadarśinah

(Bhagavad Gita 4:34)

"In the search for knowledge and wisdom, a seeker should approach the qualified guru with reverence, humble enquiries, and devoted service. Once the guru has tested and accepted the disciple, he will proceed to expound the highest Truth."

The Kularnava Tantra urges the following advice:

A disciple is also responsible for testing the credibility of the guru. There are many self-designated gurus of dubious heritage with minimal familiarity with Tantra, mantras, and the medicinal effects of plants and herbs. Their minds, full of greed and temptation, focus on exploiting the material wealth of their students. In this regard, Tantra instructs a student to quietly leave an incompetent or unworthy teacher as a bee leaves a flower devoid of honey and moves on to a new, more suitable one.

According to the Goutamiya Tantra, a worthy disciple should cultivate the following qualities:

i) A good character, free from blemish as well as a guiltless nature,

ii) Inner purity in thoughts, words, and mind,

iii) A constant drive to reach the supreme goal of life – *moksha* or liberation,

iv) Well-versed in the scriptures,

v) An intelligent attitude in order to understand the teachings of the guru, and the hidden meaning of the scriptures,

vi) A serviceful attitude towards one's parents,

vii) An inner drive to remain righteous, obedient to moral and ethical principles,

viii) Devotion and a serviceful attitude towards the guru,
ix) Good health,
x) A balanced mind,
xi) Compassion for others,
xii) A strong ability to sacrifice temporary pleasure,
xiii) An ardent and sincere desire for the spiritual path,
xiv) An attitude of constant alertness in activity,
xv) Remaining free from delusion, attachment, and envy.

The Rudra Yamala warns the guru to avoid a student who happens to be passionate, crooked, of blemished character, full of falsehood, disobedient, incompetent, extremely inadvertent, quarrelsome, attracted to sinful activities, devoid of faith, impatient, easily overpowered by anger, of debatable moral values, and other such qualities.

In ancient times, during the period of apprenticeship the student lived in an ashram with the teacher, often in a secluded forest. The constant proximity and exclusive contact with the teacher, the source of infinite knowledge, compassion, and love, enabled the student to be immersed in an attitude of obedience and service. Following the role model of discipline and self-control, the disciple became a reflection of the master's teaching.

Within the tantric scriptures there is a list of rules, which the student should follow during daily life. The following are but a few examples:

i) In the guru's presence keep the senses and mind under control;
ii) Do not sit on the guru's bed or cushion;
iii) Whenever the guru comes into sight, go forward a few steps to receive him with reverence;
iv) Serve the guru with body and mind (with physical effort and mental dedication);

v) Never visit the guru with empty hands, take at least a flower or a piece of firewood;
vi) Bow down to the guru with love and reverence, with out ego or shyness;
vii) Try to fulfill the instructions of the guru;
viii) Show reverence to all the guru's belongings;
ix) Never walk ahead of the guru; follow him with love;
x) Never sit insolently before the guru, but with a respectful attitude;
xi) When close to the guru give up falsehood, fear, idleness, useless chatter, and betrayal;
xii) Sleep after the guru has gone to bed and get up before the guru awakes.

When a disciple is ready and feels a strong desire for Self-unfoldment, God sends a guru to show the way and the student learns from the dynamic living example of the designated master. A guru becomes like a mother who provides the source of spiritual life, nourishment, and guidance through unconditional love without expectation.

Diksha

The Yogini Tantra defines initiation, *diksha,* as derived from two syllables: *di — diyate jñanam atyantam* 'imparting supreme knowledge,' and *ksha — kshiyate sarva samsayam*, 'destroying all ignorance and doubt.'

Initiation is a sacred ceremony, performed by a qualified teacher, which introduces a sincere seeker to spiritual life. The day of the *diksha* marks a spiritual transformation in a student's life, and hence has to be astrologically an auspicious day. Among all possible days for initiation, the day of a lunar eclipse has a special significance. The process of initiation into Tantra involves a rather complex procedure for both the disciple and the guru, ranging from collecting various articles to rigorous fasting for inner purification. Various tantric works enumerate different types of *diksha* rituals:

1) *Kriyavati*	the guru performs certain rituals in order to purify the body and mind of the student during initiation.
2) *Kalavati*	the guru perceives the existence of *kala,* or the power of *panchabhuta* (gross elements), such as *nivritti kala* (the power of detachment) or *vidyakala* (the power of knowledge), in the body of the disciple. He meditates on *kala* and proceeds to anoint the student.
3) *Varnamayi*	the guru infuses the spirit of *varna* (letters of the alphabet), which are associated with energy (*shakti*), in different parts of the disciple's body.
4) *Vedamayi*	the guru initiates the disciple through the power of thought.

Initiation can be performed in different ways:

i) *Sparsha diksha*	during initiation the guru touches a special part of the body like the 'third eye,' or the spine, rousing spiritual consciousness.
ii) *Vag diksha*	the guru awakens spiritual consciousness in the life of the disciple by uttering a mantra into the ear.
iii) *Drig/chakshushi diksha*	the guru infuses spiritual energy by looking intently at the disciple. This is also otherwise known as *shambhavi diksha.*

Diksha is a technical procedure that varies according to the tradition of a particular lineage. It usually encompasses many rituals such as *abhisheka* or the sprinkling of holy water on the disciple, and concludes with a Vedic or tantric fire ceremony. The simplest form of initiation is *mantra upadesha* or uttering a mantra of *ishta devata* (the chosen presiding deity) into the disciple's ear.

Ishta Devata

God is one, and has no equal. God is Absolute and manifests in varied names and forms. To worship God in symbols such as *shivalinga* or *saligrama,* or Kali, Durga, or Ganesha, is essentially worshipping the Supreme, the One. *Sadhakas* involved in tantric rituals and meditation choose the deity (*ishta devata*), most dear to them. Besides personal affinity with the deity, the choice also depends on the purpose of meditation and worship. The guru-preceptor can also choose the *ishta devata* if a seeker cannot decide on one. The *ishta devata* can be either male or female.

At first, Tantra advocates worship and meditation with a form, but eventually a devotee is encouraged to go beyond form into a more abstract phase. In tantric texts, this is described in the following way,

uttama brahma sadbhāva dhyāna bhāvastu madhyamā
stuti japo adhamo bhāvo bahih pujādhamādhama

(Mahanirvana Tantra)

"It is the supreme state to be in constant communion with the Absolute; a meditative outlook is in the middle; and chanting hymns and repeating mantras is considered primary external worship or the ground work."

For the average devotee identifying with a form in worship is much easier in the beginning stages. As progress is made on the spiritual path, meditation on the formless is encouraged and becomes a natural step forward. Shri Ramakrishna Paramahamsa started his spiritual journey by worshipping the Divine Mother. But later he learned meditation on the formless from Totapuri, the naked monk.

Each deity has one or more mantras. Some are in word-symbols called *bijakshari mantra,* the 'seed' mantra. Besides the mantra, every *ishta devata* has a list of a thousand holy names, *sahasranama,* and a *kavacha,* protective recitation that acts like a shield. All these are received ceremonially from the guru, during *diksha* or initiation.

Ishta Mantra

Etymologically, mantra means *mana* or 'mind' and *trana* or 'liberation.' Metaphorically this is interpreted as that which makes the mind free. The essence of initiation is the transmission of a mantra from the guru to the disciple. Another interpretation is *man* 'to reflect' and *tra* 'to protect,' that which offers protection to the one who reflects upon it. In this context, protection implies to be safe from harm while pursuing the path of liberation. *Mantra vidya* or *mantra shastra*, the science of mantras, offers a detailed and elaborate analysis classifying them into four categories:

1)	*Vaidiki*	if the source of the mantra is the Vedas,
2)	*Pauraniki*	mantras that originate from the Puranas,
3)	*Tantriki*	includes mantras derived from *ijakshara* or seed-syllables,
4)	*Laukiki*	all traditional mantras.

Vedic mantras are restrictive. They can be chanted by trained, qualified individuals in a proper environment and recited in a specific meter. Tantric mantras are free from such limitations. In the tradition of Tantra, a mantra is not just a letter or a combination of letters of the alphabet; it has a much deeper significance. Within the sound symbol rests the power and consciousness of the Supreme Creator, Brahman, or Its manifestation.

In classical tantric texts, Brahman is known as *svayam prakasha* or Self-effulgent. Before creation there was a state of inactivity, then there was *vimarsha* or deliberation in Brahman. From this emanated the throb or *spanda* and this in turn gave way to the first primordial sound or *nada*. *Nada* through *spanda* became dynamic and focused on a *bindu* or point. When *bindu* split in two, which is the state of *shiva-shakti* — the male and female, it was the beginning of creation, known as *sarga*.

Nada or *shabda brahman* is the spirit of the mantra. In Tantra, devotees should not only know the mantra, but also be familiar with its connotation or *mantrartha*. They should also prove able to master the art of awakening consciousness through the mantra, which is known as *mantra chaitanya*.

Tantric mantras can be classified into either *saura* (solar) or *saumya* (lunar). A mantra that enthralls energy is solar, whereas the one that brings peace is lunar. Mantras can also be divided into three categories: masculine, feminine, and neuter. Masculine and neuter mantras are referred to as mantras, but feminine mantras are called *vidyas* such as *shri vidya, dasha maha vidya*, and such. Another way of identifying them is by their ending. Those ending with *hum, vasat,* or *phat* are masculine mantras; those ending in *svaha* and *vaushat* are feminine; ones ending in *namah* are neuter.

Mantras can be monosyllabic or multi-syllabic. Monosyllabic mantras like *klim,* or *hrim* are also known as *bija* (seed) *mantras* or *bijakshara*. Just as a seed has a tremendous hidden potential to manifest and grow into a mighty tree under the right conditions, so has the *bija mantra*. It produces *siddhi,* perfection and revelation, if used under the instructions of a qualified teacher. Although many mantras can be found in books, they should not be used unless transmitted by the guru. Tantra prescribes many ways to invoke and arouse the power of a mantra to increase its effectiveness:

1) *Upavasa sharira shodhana*	fasting and purification of the body,
2) *Chakra shodhana*	purification of the chakras,
3) *Nadi shodhana*	purification of the *pranic* channels,
4) *Mukha shodhana*	purification of the mouth,
5) *Jihva shodhana*	purification of the tongue,
6) *Ashauca bhanga*	elimination of impurity,
7) *Nidra bhanga*	arousal from slumber.

Japa

A guru should instruct his disciples on how to chant and concentrate in order to get the maximum benefit from the use of a mantra. *Japa* (repetition of a mantra) can also be defined as the process to become free from rebirth; *ja* is derived from *janma* and *pa* from *papa*, which means to attain liberation through the elimination of impurities.

The repetition of a mantra in a prescribed manner can be of three types:

i)	*Vachika*	*uccha*	audible with rhythm,
ii)	*Upamsu*	*madhya*	a whisper, or by silent movement of the lips,
iii)	*Manasa*	*manda*	mental repetition of the words.

While performing *japa*, a devotee follows the consecutive number of invocations using the fingers (*kara mala*) or with a rosary (*japa mala*). These practices vary depending on the occasion and the selected deity. There is a subtle way of chanting known as *ajapa japa*, which literally means 'non-chanting chants,' when *japa* occurs automatically with no effort from the devotee. The average human being, following a moderate routine, breaths approximately 21,600 times in 24 hours, some extraordinary yogis and tantrics have been known to use a mantra with every breath.

Tantra describes *purascarana* as an important system of *japa,* associated with ritualistic practices. *Purascarana* means *puras* 'before' and *caran,* 'performing' or 'carrying' or 'progressing'.

There are several meanings involved:

1) Perfection of a procedure before taking action,
2) Through devotion, the chosen deity is a source of inspiration and blessings,
3) The spiritual aspirant advances to the state before Creation.

Purascarana has several constituents:

i) *Japa* repetition of a mantra in a prescribed manner,
ii) *Dhyana* meditation,
iii) *Puja* ritualistic worship,
iv) *Homa* oblations into a duly consecrated fire,
v) *Tarpana* ceremonial offering of water satiating the chosen deity,
vi) *Brahmana bhojana* 'Feeding the *Brahmana,*' thus joining good conduct with due procedure.

Some tantric works recommend the repetition of a mantra 240 million times. One tenth (24 million) should be offered as oblations, one tenth of oblations should be in the form of *tarpana,* one tenth of *tarpana* should be done as *abhisheka*, and one tenth of this, is the number of Brahmins that should be fed. If a devotee cannot accomplish all of these steps, then the number of chantings should be doubled.

When *purascarana* is performed in a holy place or during an auspicious time, like the *navaratras* (nine days in March–April or September–October) or during a solar or a lunar eclipse, it is believed to be extremely effective.

Kundalini and the Chakras

As mentioned previously, Brahman and Shakti, *purusha* and *prakriti,* Shiva and Parvati are two aspects of One Truth. The external world manifests through Shakti (Prakriti) associated with Brahman.

The Bhagavad Gita (9:10) describes it in the following way,

mayādhyakṣeṇa prakrtiḥ sūyate sacarācaram
hetunānena kaunteya jagad viparcivartate

"O son of Kunti! With me as the supervisor, divine nature produces all things animate and inanimate. This is the cause of the universe."

The manifestation of the external world is the play of *shakti* or *prakriti.* Similarly, *kundalini* is the source of untapped energy stored in the body of each human being and constitutes the source of basic energy. It is generally portrayed as a coiled serpent or serpent-power remaining hidden in the *mula padma* or *muladhara chakra* at the base of the spine. There are however, many divergent experiences about the exact location of the *kundalini*. According to the interpretation of certain realized masters, including my own Gurudev, *kundalini* is not located at the base of the spine, but in the brain, which is the store-house of energy and the source of all play in the physical, mental, and spiritual realms. Through the guidance of a realized master, a seeker should tap the unexplored energy in the brain.

According to tantric texts there are three *nadis* or pranic canals in the spine, that allow life's energy to flow from the brain down to the bottom of the spine. The central canal is called the *sushumna,* to the left lies the *ida* and to the right the *pingala.* Both the *ida* and *pingala* canals are inter-twined inside the spinal column. Each chakra, or nerve plexus, becomes a place of mutual conjunction.

Chakra literally means disc or wheel. It is also known as lotus or *padma* (lotus pose). There are many chakras, but seven are paramount in spiritual practice. The seven major chakras are the centers for the play of consciousness. Their location is more psychological than physical. The *muladhara chakra* is at the base of the spine, the *svadhisthana chakra* is behind the genitals, the *manipura chakra* is at the back of the navel, the *anahata chakra* corresponds to the middle of the chest, the *vishuddha chakra* is in the throat, the *ajna chakra* is located mid-point between the eyebrows; and the *sahasrara chakra* is at the top of the head.

The chakras are portrayed as lotuses with varying numbers of petals, colours and letters corresponding to specific mantras. (See Table 1, page 48.) *Kundalini* and the chakras bridge the two paths of Tantra and Yoga, since both schools elaborately utilize these two fundamental and mystical concepts.

Summary

Tantra finds its roots in the Vedas and is not at odds with Vedic principles and morality. It has evolved as a simplified form of Vedic philosophy that is accessible to everyone regardless of race, caste, or creed. Tantra is a beautiful combination of Vedantic truth and Samkhya principles, the latter being the philosophy that deals with cosmic evolution and the principle of cause and effect. Tantrics drew from several disciplines to develop practical and verifiable methods to accelerate spiritual evolution.

The most important concept in Tantra is the necessity of unifying opposites in order to attain enlightenment. These opposites are usually represented as Shiva (consciousness) and *shakti* (energy); *purusha* (the soul) and *prakriti* (nature); male and female. The union of both is required for the highest level of understanding. These polar opposites are in reality one, this is the ultimate truth of Tantra.

An important tantric concept, which will be discussed more in Part II, is that of the equality of macrocosm and microcosm. According to this principle everything in the external universe is also represented internally, in the body of every individual; the same forces (*gunas*) govern both.

An essential prerequisite to the practice of Tantra is the guidance of a competent guru who can initiate the aspirant into the correct methods of its application. A qualified guru is one who has experienced the discipline directly and has achieved various stages of spiritual development. Qualities essential for both teachers and students are carefully described in the scriptures.

The Vedas, created in Sanskrit, are the sound-manifestation of the Absolute or the Supreme. Through the use of mantra, meditation, and concentration, the *kundalini shakti* can be aroused from the base of the spine and gradually brought up through the *sushumna* channel to the *sahasrara* or thousand-petal lotus at the crown of the head. When the mind becomes highly purified, through profound meditation and intense devotion, the spiritual aspirant experiences the ultimate bliss, the union of Shiva and Shakti, attaining permanent liberation.

The following metaphorical explanation of a rare Sanskrit text, Jñana Sankalini Tantra, is aimed at accelerating the spiritual progress of sincere seekers who wish to follow the inward journey for spiritual evolution through contemplation and meditation.

PART II

Jnana Sankalini Tantra: A Dialogue Between Shiva & Parvathi

Introduction

Tantric texts can be classified into two categories, some include ritualistic practices and others concentrate on esoteric and metaphysical wisdom. Jñana Sankalini Tantra clearly belongs to the second category. Most tantric texts are basically records of the timeless dialogue between Shiva and Parvati. This book is centered on a conversation between Lord Shiva and his divine consort, Parvati, and it extends to 110 verses.

According to Hindu mythology, Lord Shiva is the Supreme Yogi, a highly accomplished ascetic who dwells atop the icy peaks of the Himalayas, with his divine consort, Parvati, his chief disciple. Lord Shiva is considered to be the master of Tantra, Yoga, Music, Dance, and Phonetics. He shares his vast knowledge with Parvati in response to her earnest enquiries.

Jñana Sankalini Tantra is considered the Path of Knowledge. The word *jñana* represents 'knowledge,' but true knowledge is not easy to acquire because it demands discipline and sincere effort. Knowledge, once attained, needs to be maintained.

In Sanskrit it is said, *anabhyāse viṣam vidyām*:

"Knowledge without practice is useless."

The word *sankalini* is derived from the root word *kalana* or 'enumeration,' 'comprehension,' or 'assessment,' and *samkalana,* which means 'complete' or 'concise.' Thus, Jñana Sankalini is a complete or concise treaty on Tantra. The text itself is unique in its approach and explanation as it is based on internal worship and meditation rather than external ritualistic practice. Like many tantric scriptures it is extremely subtle in nature, so it requires a sharp mind and intellect to comprehend the hidden depth of its message.

This metaphorical explanation of such a rare Sanskrit text is aimed at accelerating the spiritual progress of sincere seekers, who wish to follow the inward journey for spiritual evolution through contemplation and meditation.

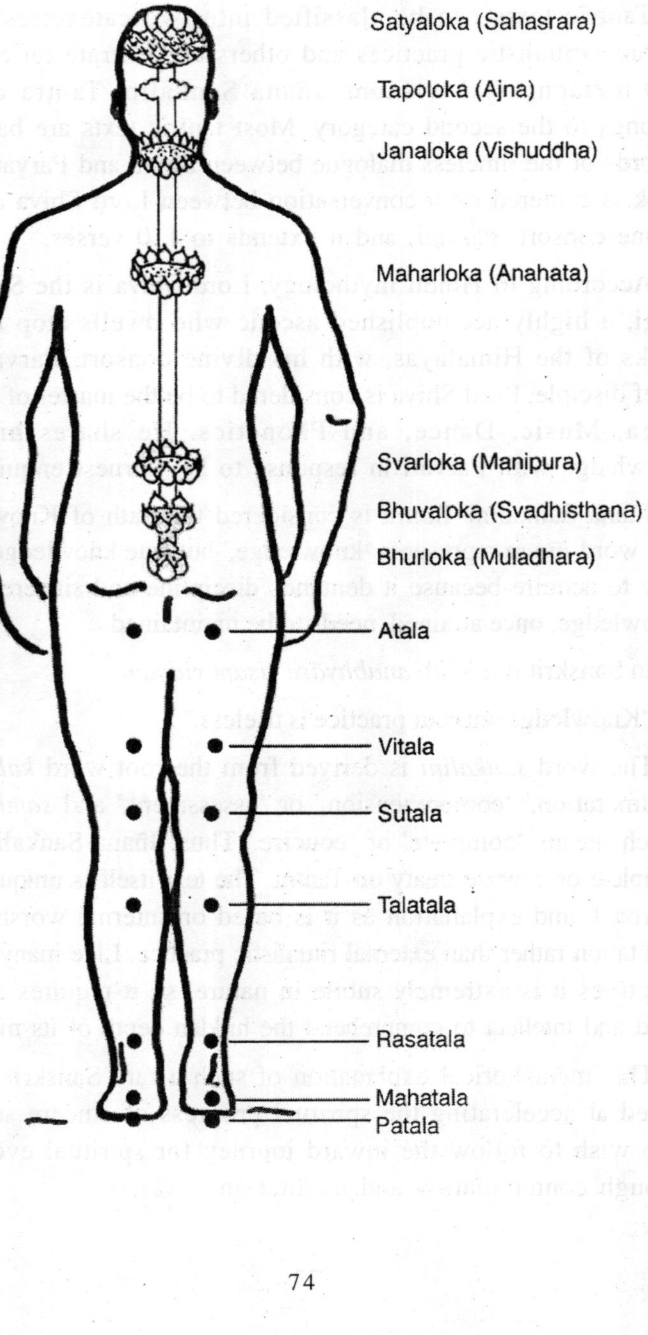
Satyaloka (Sahasrara)
Tapoloka (Ajna)
Janaloka (Vishuddha)
Maharloka (Anahata)
Svarloka (Manipura)
Bhuvaloka (Svadhisthana)
Bhurloka (Muladhara)
Atala
Vitala
Sutala
Talatala
Rasatala
Mahatala
Patala

Verse 1

kailāsa śikharāsīnam
devadeva jagadgurum
pṛcchati sma mahādevī
brūhi jñānaṃ maheśvara

Translation

On the top of Mount Kailasha, Mahadevi (Parvati) asked Jagadguru Lord Shiva, "O Maheshwara, or Supreme Lord, please reveal to me what is *jñanam* (knowledge)."

Metaphorical Interpretation

Besides the literal or apparent meaning within the ancient spiritual text there are many inner connotations with deep spiritual and practical significance. They are applicable to every day life and become guidelines in the spiritual path. It is the practical aspect that makes the scriptures all the more valuable.

Throughout the ages the Himalayas, in northern India, have become the chosen site for the practice of spiritual paths leading to Self-realization. These vast mountain ranges, extending over hundreds of miles, are the source of many magnificent rivers of enormous religious and spiritual significance, such as the Ganga, the Yamuna, the Sindhu, the Brahmaputra, and many others. Lay pilgrims or spiritual seekers have dipped into these rivers.

Mount Kailasha, the Himalayan range, and Lake Manasarovar are prominent places of pilgrimage for the Hindus, and have attracted many a spiritual seeker for eons. Despite the tremendous physical strain and risks of traversing the rugged mountains, devotees and spiritual seekers are drawn to this sacred spot in order to experience divine ecstasy. Ancient mythological Hindu texts are rife with descriptions of Mount Kailasha, and its spiritual significance.

According to these texts Lord Shiva, with his consort, Parvati, and their two sons, Ganesha and Kartikeya live on Mount Kailasha. Shiva is one of the three main deities of the sacred Hindu trinity: Brahma, Vishnu, and Shiva, respectively the creator, the sustainer, and the dissolver of the universe.

Ancient mythology describes Shiva as the originator and propagator of divine wisdom: Tantra, Yoga, Music, Dance, Grammar, and Language. Shiva is the Supreme Master of Tantra, Yoga, and meditation; teaching the art of discrimination and detachment from his own experience. Shiva remains permanently engrossed in a state of deep meditation, experiencing divine bliss.

There is a scriptural dictum, *jñānam maheśvarāt icchet*: "seek divine knowledge from Maheshwara." Maheshwara consists of two words: *maha* and *Ishwara*. *Maha* means 'great' or 'supreme' and *Ishwara* means 'Lord' or 'master of prosperity.' One who has thorough control over the senses, mind, and ego is Maheshwara or the Supreme Lord. To realize Shiva, a devotee must climb Mount Kailasha, his divine abode.

In the spiritual context, there is a direct correlation between the human body and the universe. Just as Mount Kailasha is situated in the north, in the high hills of the Himalayas, the spiritual Kailasha, in every individual, is located in the fontanel, at the *sahasrara* or the crown of the head, known as the seventh chakra in both yogic and tantric texts.

The word *Kailasha* is composed of several Sanskrit letters: *ka, i, la, a, sha. Ka* represents Brahman, *i* stands for *shakti* or 'energy,' *la* is *laya* or 'dissolution,' *a* is 'the first primordial sound' and *sha* is *shira* or 'the head.' Combined together, *Kailasha* means the place where one realizes the formless Brahman, manifested as divine energy. In this inner sanctum all the propensities of the mind dissolve, and one can hear the divine sound *Om* (*a u m*), beginning with the sacred letter *a*. This place is located at the crown of the head. The word Himalaya consists of two words, *hima* — 'cold,' 'frigid,' 'frosty,' and *alaya* — 'abode,' 'house,' 'dwelling,' or 'place,' 'a place of coolness and calmness.' North pole in the human body is at the top of the head and south pole is at the feet. There are many suitable places in the body apt for concentration and meditation. Among them, the mid-point of the eyebrows and the fontanel, known as the 'cave of the cranium,' are considered the most favorable in spiritual terms. Focusing at either of these points helps dissolve restless propensities, such as anger, ego, and vanity. A state of inner calmness is achieved. Each human head has a potential to be the Himalaya, a place of coolness and calmness. Consciousness and energy can be raised from the lower centers, through the spine, to the very peak of Mount Kailasha. Meditation is a tool that enables the spiritual seeker to transform life into a haven of tranquility, peace, and joy.

In the first verse, Mahadevi (Parvati), the divine consort, is described as seated on Mount Kailasha (the *sahasrara chakra),* seeking knowledge from Shiva, her beloved Lord and master; object of her devotion. Parvati represents the power of consciousness in every person, embodying the disciple, whereas Shiva is the Supreme Self, the divine preceptor. Parvati is the daughter of Parvata, 'the mountain,' Himalaya, a symbol of 'strength,' 'determination,' and 'unshakable faith.' Since Parvati is an ardent follower of her master, she demonstrates her sincerity and devotion through self-enquiry and intent to incorporate Shiva's teachings in practical life.

The Proper Way to Enquire

A spiritual journey is a four-fold path of self-evolution. A true spiritual seeker should:

1) Have a burning desire for spiritual progress,
2) Seek the company of upright and virtuous people and become familiar with the scriptures,

3) Undertake a sincere spiritual practice under the guidance of a teacher,

4) Strive to attain Self-realization.

Devotees that feel a deep desire for spiritual evolution should seek the guidance of a master and gain essential knowledge needed to tread the spiritual path. Ego is a barrier in this path. Spiritual seekers should humbly approach the master equipped with the necessary qualifications and put forth their questions with the sole purpose of gaining understanding. A truly spiritual mind is free from doubts, and full of calmness. For every valid question, there is a valid answer. Some people, however, make the repeated mistake of asking questions saturated with ego, so as to exhibit their own knowledge. The type of questions asked by disciples in general, fall under two categories:

1) Judgmental questions — In the same way that a teacher poses questions to assess a student's intelligence and comprehension, a disciple may pose questions to judge the guru's competence and trustworthiness.

2) Search for knowledge — Questions are asked with sincere devotion and determination to gain spiritual insight. Such enquiry arises from the heart with the desire for self-unfoldment. When a student is ready, God will send a befitting teacher to impart inner knowledge and dissolve the darkness of ignorance.

In the Bhagavad Gita (4:34) the Lord says,

tad viddhi praṇipātena paripraśnena sevayā
upadekṣyanti te jñānaṃ jñāninastattvadarśinah

"To gain knowledge of the Absolute, approach a spiritual master. Prostrate with love, surrender, and serve the teacher. Ask proper questions with love and humility. Then the teacher imparts knowledge, as he has the inner experience."

Parvati, sitting at the feet of Shiva, prays, "O Lord of lords, teacher of the universe, Maheshwara, please kindle the flame of knowledge in me so that the darkness of ignorance and doubt may disappear."

Devadeva is a compound word, meaning 'God of gods' or 'Lord of lords'. Many who lack proper understanding of Hindu spiritual traditions consider such phrases to imply polytheism (the worship of more than one god). But, in reality, in spiritual Hindu tradition there is only one God (Brahman, neither male nor female, but of neutral gender), who manifests in varied forms. One of the Vedas maintains, *ekaṃ sat viprāḥ bahudā vadanti*: "Scholars speak of One Truth in different modes."

Diverse Manifestations of the Supreme Self

There is only One cosmic principle, Brahman or the Absolute, permeating this entire creation. So each part of the human body, every sense organ has a *deva* (illumined one) as a presiding deity. These deities are described as god with a small 'g,' commanding various organs of action and perception.

Ear	Digdevata (deity of space)
Skin	Vayu (deity of the air element)
Eye	Surya (the sun god. According to some sages, the left eye, the right eye and the third eye are the abode of the moon, the sun, and of fire)
Tongue	Varuna (deity of the water element)
Nose	Ashwini Kumaras (the twin deities considered the celestial 'physicians')
Speech organ	Agni (deity of fire)
Hands	Indra (deity of rain)
Feet	Vishnu (deity of sustenance, the second main god belonging to the Hindu trinity)

Anus	Yama (deity of death, virtue, and judgment)
Genitals	Prajapati (deity of birth and creation)
Mind	Chandra (the moon god)
Intellect	Brahma (deity of Creation; the first main god composing the sacred Hindu trinity)
Ego (*Ahamkara*)	Rudra (an epithet for Shiva, representing anger)
Memory (*Citta*)	Vasudeva (an epithet of Vishnu)
Muladhara (coccyx)	Ganesha (the god of knowledge and success)
Svadhisthana (sacral)	Devi, Durga, Kali, and others (goddess of strength and creativity)
Manipura (navel)	Surya/Agni(sun god/god of fire)
Anahata (dorsal)	Vishnu/Narayana (god as a symbol of life energy)
Vishuddha (cervical)	Shiva (deity of destruction and dissolution; third main god composing the sacred Hindu trinity)

Devadeva, 'God of all gods' or 'the indwelling Self,' is the innermost source of illumination to all other *devas* (gods); the Supreme Spirit, whose energy and strength activate all beings.

Jagadguru means the 'guru' or 'master' of *jagat* or 'the universe.' The etymological meaning of *jagat* is 'repeatedly oscillating phenomena.' The universe is constantly evolving and so does the human body. The indwelling Self is the real teacher but the universe (*jagat*) becomes an extensive research center. Each human life is designed for the purpose of learning and experiencing Truth within. God manifests as a teacher, through many names and forms. God is the *Jagadguru.* When a person is ready to absorb sacred knowledge, it will come in varied forms.

Maheshwara means Supreme Lord. As stated earlier, the word is derived from two Sanskrit terms, *maha* or 'great' or 'supreme' and *Ishwara* or 'lord.' In each of the seven chakras located in the spine, the presence of divinity is described respectively as Visva (*Muladhara*), Virat (*Svadhisthana*), Taijas (*Manipura*), Hiranyagarbha (*Anahata*), Ishwara (*Vishuddha*), Prajna (*Ajna*), and Maheshwara (*Sahasrara*). The abode of God is therefore the seat of Maheshwara, or the Supreme Lord.

A worthy disciple inherits the spiritual treasure from one's own guru. Wisdom is a blessing that can only be acquired through a mixture of strong yearning, humility, devotion, and service. A guru is ever compassionate, ready to bestow to a sincere disciple the spiritual heritage already in one's possession. In this verse, it is clear that Parvati, as recipient, has the right attitude. She does not see Shiva as an ordinary husband, but perceiving divinity in him, she prays with deep love and concentration in order to experience the taste of the divine nectar of wisdom.

Celestial beings are referred to as *deva (m)* or *devi (f)*. Parvati, portrayed as a *devi*, represents a sincere disciple filled with a burning desire for self-evolvement. *Deva* and *devi* are both derived from the root word *div* meaning 'illumination,' 'brilliance,' and 'light.' When the restless mind is trained to be tranquil, through the practice of meditation and breath control, a level of superconsciousness is attained and a devotee is able to experience inner light (*antarjyoti*), at the crown of the head, and in all the sense organs.

sarvadvāreṣu kaunteya prakāśa upajāyate

(Bhagavad Gita 14:11)

The Lord says, "O Son of Kunti (Arjuna), in every door (of the body) divine illumination manifests."

Verse 2

devī uvāca
kutaḥ sṛṣṭir bhavet deva
kathaṃ sṛṣṭi vinaśyati
brahmajñānaṃ kathaṃ deva
sṛṣṭi samhāra varjitam

Translation

Devi asked, "From where does creation manifest, O Lord, and how does it dissolve? What is *brahmajñanam* (knowledge of the Absolute), which is devoid of creation and dissolution?"

Metaphorical Interpretation

Creation is a cosmic mystery. Scientists of the physical world, equipped with tools and analytical observation; philosophers using their intellect as a tool; saints, sages, and mystics, through deep meditation, have all, in their own way, tried to solve the mystery of creation. Yet the clear sky in the darkness of night, with myriads of shining bright stars, reminds us again and again that the human mind is limited and cannot readily grasp the mystery of creation. God is infinite, and creation is extremely vast, complex, and beyond human comprehension.

Divergent multidimensional views of creation are controversial, even contradictory. Ancient scriptures such as the Vedas and the Upanishads have themselves varied theories of creation and the evolutionary process. In this verse, Parvati, embodying the role of a seeker, portrays the inner quest in each person:

i) How did creation begin?
ii) How does creation come to an end?
iii) How is knowledge of Brahman (the Absolute), itself beyond creation and dissolution, attained?

In the subsequent verses, Lord Shiva answers these questions in detail. It forms the vital foundation for the superstructure of divine knowledge. The three basic concepts in this verse are: *srishti* (creation), *vinasha* (destruction, dissolution), and *brahmajñana* (knowledge of the Absolute; ultimate wisdom).

***Srishti* (creation)**

This word is derived from the root word *srj,* which consists of three letters *sa, ra,* and *ja. Sa* means 'the Soul' or 'God,' *ra* means 'movement' or 'vibration'; and *ja* means 'manifestation,' 'materialization,' or 'to be born.' The three together imply that creation is the vibratory manifestation of the Soul or God. Every form of creation is a vibration of cosmic energy; speech is the creation of sound through the vibration of the vocal cords in a specific way, and thought is also a product of vibration in the ocean of the mind.

***Vinasha* (complete dissolution)**

This concept is divided into two: *vi* means 'perfect' or 'complete,' whereas *nasha* means 'destruction,' 'disappearance,' or 'dissolution.' Every beginning has an end; as every creation, in turn, is destroyed. Dissolution is 'perfect disappearance,' i.e., the creative energy merges into the Supreme. A temporary disappearance occurs when we sleep, we lose consciousness of ourselves and of the surrounding world. Finally, what comes from the Absolute will return to the Absolute.

***Brahmajñana* (knowledge of the Absolute)**

Ignorance is darkness; knowledge is light. Human growth is directed towards knowledge from childhood to adulthood and is repeated in life after life. A child from early on in life shows a great eagerness to know what happens around him. "The why of a child is the key to philosophy," it is said. Knowledge is classified in two groups, *aparavidya* (material knowledge) and *paravidya* (supreme knowledge) (Mundaka Upanishad 1:1:4).

Material knowledge (*aparavidya*), is acquired through the use of the five sense organs of perception: eyes (sight), ears (hearing), nose (smell), tongue (taste), and skin (touch), together with the help of the four internal instruments; mind, intellect, ego, and memory. The peripheral knowledge is expanded by the use of the elasticity and curiosity, inherent to the mind, the faulty memory, and the intellect's capacity for analysis. In Sanskrit, this process is described as *paroksha-jñana,* or 'the indirect means to gain knowledge.' If the senses or the mind are not in a healthy state, the acquisition of knowledge will be skewed and the result flawed.

Spiritual wisdom (*paravidya*), on the other hand, can only be gained through *a-paroksha anubhuti* or 'direct experience.' Supreme Truth is revealed to a sincere seeker once one has disciplined the senses and cleansed and purified the mind through deep meditation, and devout prayer. A profound awareness of communion with God manifests in Absolute Knowledge, a revelation of light unfolding itself from inner experience.

In the Bhagavad Gita (6:22) the Lord teaches,

yaṃ labdhvā cāparaṃ lābhaṃ manyate nādhikaṃ tatah
yasmin sthito na dukhena guruṇāpi vicālyate

"One who gains that beyond which there is no greater, and remains established (in it), is not moved (even) by the greatest sorrow."

Spiritual knowledge or *paravidya* dispels ignorance and frees an individual from the bondage of pleasure and pain, birth and death. This state of pure mind, complete equilibrium, and equanimity can only be achieved through self-discipline. Knowledge becomes the gateway to liberation. To live in pure knowledge, immersed in a state of constant awareness, is to live in God.

Verse 3

īśvara uvāca
avyaktāt ca bhavet sṛṣṭiḥ
avyaktaṃ ca vinaśyati
avyaktaṃ brahmaṇo jñānam
sṛṣṭi saṃhāra varjitam

Translation

Ishwara replied, "Creation comes from *avyakta* (the unmanifested) and leads to *avyakta* (dissolution). *Avyaktam* is *brahmajñanam* (knowledge of the Absolute), devoid of creation and dissolution."

Metaphorical Interpretation

Some world religions maintain that God is formless and some teach that God has form. In the Vedic teaching the formless God is known as Brahman, beyond all attributes and qualities, beyond creation and dissolution, while Ishwara is the manifested aspect of God. Perceived within creation Ishwara is the Supreme Soul, represented here by Lord Shiva.

The Taittiriya Upanishad (2:1:3) gives a very lucid and exhaustive description of the process of creation. Creation is the manifestation of a subtle element into its gross form. The Supreme Soul manifested in space, then in air, fire, water, and finally, in the earth. Life emerged in sequence from plants and trees to animals and humans. The entire creation is nothing but a manifestation of the Absolute.

In the Gita (2:28), the Lord says,

avyaktādīni bhūtāni vyaktamadhyāni bhārata
avyakta nidhanānyeva tatra kā paridevanā

"Beings are *avyakta,* un-manifested, in the beginning, *vyakta,* manifested in the middle and *avyakta,* un-manifested again at the end. O Bharata (Arjuna), what is the cause for grief?"

Further on, in the Gita (4:3), Lord Krishna offers the following explanation,

mama yonirmahadbrahma tasmin garbhaṃ dadāmyaham
sambhava sarvabhūtānāṃ tato bhavati bhārata

"Great Brahma (*prakriti*) is my womb. In that I cast the seed, and from it sprout all beings, O Bharata (Arjuna)."

Avyakta, in Sanskrit, has multiple meanings.Among them are:

1) Indivisible, imperceptible, un-manifest,
2) Primary matter with no shape,
3) Name of Vishnu as well as Shiva,
4) Supreme Being, Universal Spirit, Brahman,
5) The primary germ of Nature, the earliest productive principle,
6) The Soul,
7) Indistinct, apparent,
8) Undeveloped, uncreated.

The cycle of un-manifest, manifest, back to un-manifest is often illustrated in scriptures through an analogy of a piece of jewelry made from a lump of gold. That is the principle of creation. When the piece of jewelry becomes old or outdated, the goldsmith just melts it into gold. This is dissolution.

According to the Vedas, every creation is the result of two causes, known as:

nimitta karana (the efficient cause) — the skill or the talent involved in the process of creation,

upadana karana (the material cause) — the instruments as

well as other materials involved in shaping an object.

In the Mundaka Upanishad (1:1:7), the process of creation is explained by the prototype of the spider and its web. A spider's web is a very fine net-like structure spun from its own saliva. The spider lives in it, traps its prey, and finally rolls up the cobweb into a ball and swallows it. The spider creates, maintains, and destroys the web of its own creation. This model is relevant because the spider is the efficient as well as the material cause. God is the creator and created the universe out of Itself. The creative aspect of God is called *avyakta,* or the un-manifested source. Whatever is created, under any name or form, is nothing but the manifestation of God alone, from formless to form and again into formless. It is in this context that the Upanishad declares, *sarvam khalvidam brahma:* "Everything is Brahman."

Many Hindu festivals and rituals reflect the same philosophical principle. Among the popular deities are Durga and Ganesh. In the fall season, September and October, when the crops are gathered, Hindus celebrate their annual holy rituals. Artists make and decorate clay images of the deities, in varied sizes, for ritual worship of seven to ten days. At an auspicious time at the beginning of the festival, priests perform *prana-pratishtha,* a ceremony invoking and establishing the life-principle into the idols. Thousands of devotees offer their love and devotion to their cherished deities manifested in the idol. At the end of the festival, priests celebrate the *visarjan* ceremony — or the dissipation of the life-principle. The idols are taken in a procession with great fanfare and immersed in the water of a nearby river, where they become dissolved into clay again. The source of the un-manifested state is clay *(avyakta),* the intermediate or manifested state is the creation of the idol *(vyakta),* and dissolution takes place when the idol is merged back into clay *(avyakta).*

From the 'formless' apparent 'form' comes, but 'formlessness' remains the reality. One cannot exist without the other; without a formless element, form is not possible. The middle stage is when form and formless come together, as manifested in the creation of plants, animals, and human beings.

The waves and the ocean are another example. The waves are born in the ocean, lap back and forth but eventually merge back into the ocean. The ocean alone remains unchanged. Likewise *vyakta* (creation) starts in *avyakta* (the un-manifested stage) and is dissolved back to *avyakta* (a return to the un-manifested source).

Human life unfolds as an intermediate play of *vyakta* (the manifested stage), but beneath there is a continuous flow of *avyakta* (that which is un-manifested). Each creation is a mixture of *vyakta* and *avyakta* (body and soul). The human body has a beginning and an end, but the soul remains immortal. Knowledge of *avyakta* is the culmination of Self-knowledge, dispelling all ignorance and fear. The direct experience of Truth is the most transcendental experience for a human being.

The concept of creation is an enigma but once the mystery of life is unveiled, a person will become liberated from the fear of birth and death. This is the meaning of immortality. The principle of *vyakta* teaches that if there is creation there is dissolution, but the overriding principle of *avyakta* explains that basically there is no change at all. A gold ornament has a beginning and an end, but the essence of the gold remains the same, no matter what shape it takes.

Verse 4

omkārāt akṣarāt sarvāḥ
tvetā vidyā caturdaśa
mantra pujā tapo dhyānam
karmākarma tathaiva ca

Translation

Omkara (the letter aum) is imperishable and encompasses all the fourteen vidyas (fourteen branches of knowledge), along with the six spiritual practices of chanting, worship, penance, meditation, action, and inaction.

Metaphorical Interpretation

Aum is not a word but a symbol, a sound, which is sometimes represented as *Om*. Ordinary people chant it, but tạntrics and yogis listen to the sacred sound while immersed in a meditative state.

Om is *namabrahma*	the name of God (the Formless, Absolute Brahman).
Om is *shabdabrahma*	the manifestation of the Absolute through sound.
Om is *nadabrahma*	the cosmic vibration, which is a continuous spontaneous, uninterrupted sound experienced in deep meditation.

In the Yoga Sutras of Patañjali, *aum* is described as a representation of the Absolute.

Knowledge of the sound is the beginning of revelation, the door to inner awakening. *Om*, as the primordial sound, filled with a vibrating energy, is the cause of every action. Creation started with the sound, survives with the sound, will dissolve in the sound.

In every religion, there is the use of a sacred sound syllable, like *aum, amen,* and *amin*. *Omkara,* otherwise called *aum,* is the holy syllable chanted in the beginning and at the end of the Hindu scriptures, ritualistic worship, mantras, and prayers. In the Gita (8:13) it states, *om iti ekākṣara brahma*: "The single syllable *aum* is Brahman." In the Holy Bible, there is the description of word and sound, "In the beginning was the Word, and the Word was with God, and the Word was God" (John 1:1).

The term *akshara* entails two separate concepts; the first refers to imperishable letters of the Sanskrit alphabet, the second indicates the totality of all sounds. In the Sanskrit alphabet, *a—* is the first letter, *ksha—* the last and *ra—* is the root mantra for 'fire.' The meaning of *akshara* is 'the beginning and the end'; 'the alpha and the omega.' Every sound produced is like 'fire,' with the capacity of burning ignorance if used in the right way, and creating damage and chaos if used in the wrong way.

Here in verse four, Lord Shiva explains to Parvati, that *omkara* is *akshara. Akshara* has multiple interpretations: it is imperishable, indestructible, undeceiving; it is firm, fixed, unalterable; it also represents the entire cosmos through Brahma, Vishnu, Shiva; it also represents Brahman, the Absolute; it is also a letter in the alphabet; it connotes sound, word, or speech.

The Lord continues, "O Parvati, from this divine sound *aum* comes all knowledge. In addition to this, it is also the source of *mantra, puja, tapas, dhyana, karma, and akarma.*" There are six types of practices obligatory for householders and seekers:

Mantra	Vedic hymns, prayers,
Puja	adoration, ritualistic worship,
Tapas	penance, religious austerity, mortification,
Dhyana	contemplation, reflection, meditation,
Karma	religious rights, moral duty, practice, and training,
Akarma	absence of necessary observances, inaction, realization.

Lord Shiva teaches Parvati the secret spiritual wisdom of deep meditation. Through meditation, the mind is cleansed, is gifted with the faculty of discrimination, becomes free from negatives, and is established in Truth.

Vidya

Vidya means knowledge. The scriptures define this kind of higher knowledge as the gateway to liberation. People fall into the clutches of fear, suffering, and misery out of ignorance but once darkness disappears, a devotee is able to lead a life of discrimination, understanding, and love. At this stage, life becomes fully enjoyable and ceases to be a burden. The fourteen stages of *vidya* are elaborated in the next verse.

Verse 5

ṣaḍaṇga veda catvāri
mīmāmsā nyāya vistaraḥ
dharmaśāstra purāṇāni
etā vidyā caturdaśam

Translation

The four Vedas (Rig, Yajur, Sama, Atharva*),* the six limbs of the Vedas (Shadanga) as well as the four remaining steps (Mimamsa, Nyaya, Dharma-Shastra and the Puranas*),* constitute the fourteen types of *vidya.*

Metaphorical Interpretation

In ancient times, when there were no books, pupils could only learn by listening to their guru, who was the only reliable source of material and spiritual knowledge. Spiritual knowledge was only handed down to students when one became an apprentice to a qualified teacher. A disciple would join the guru's ashram, in a quiet corner of a forest, and dedicate many years to the gradual acquisition of knowledge. This system of learning is called direct association and it has proved, through the ages, to be highly practical and beneficial in regard to spiritual growth.

Nevertheless, the study of the scriptures and related topics can only be supplementary to inner experience gained through practice. In modern times, there is an explosion of information that is often contradictory and overwhelming. By using the sense organs, especially sight and hearing, an individual enlarges the periphery of one's experience and knowledge. Such learning as a means of acquiring knowledge has several shortcomings. First, the limited nature of books cannot convey a subject entirely, since there is a deeper level that can only be grasped through analysis, contemplation, and meditation after which one arrives at the ultimate stage of comprehensive wisdom. Second, unless scriptural knowledge is applied in daily life, it is useless and becomes instrumental in raising a person's ego. Finally, words and books cannot answer all the questions that arise in the mind of a spiritual seeker. In modern society, people are mostly interested in material wealth and fail to realize that Self-realization, although intangible, is a rare treasure.

Vidya is the beginning and the end; the means as well as the goal. Elaborating the path of knowledge, Shiva explains each of the fourteen steps: the four Vedas, Rig, Yajur, Sama, and Atharva; the Shadanga (six limbs or auxiliaries of the Vedas), Siksha, Chandas, Vyakaranam, Nirukta, Jyotisha and Kalpa; and the four steps, Mimamsa, Nyaya, Dharmashastra, and the Puranas.

Vedas

The four Vedas are called Rig, Yajur, Sama, and Atharva.

Rig	The first Veda is devoted to praising the glory of God. It really means to utter every word as a mantra using speech with love and devotion.
Yajur	The second Veda addresses the need (through countless inner connotations) of reaching union with God, at every step of life.

Sama	The third Veda illustrates the state of inner harmony and self-discipline required for advancement in spiritual life.
Atharva	The fourth Veda is dedicated to achieving unending happiness and bliss while experiencing divinity. It brings about mental and astral purification.
Shadanga	Comprises the six limbs or auxiliaries of the Vedas, described as Siksha, Chandas, Vyakaranam, Nirukta, Jyotisha, and Kalpa.
Siksha	It is the science of proper articulation and pronunciation in the fields of instruction and training. Metaphorically, it is the acquisition of knowledge through the path of self-discipline and meditation.
Chandas	It is the study of prosody (verse forms and poetic meters) or material science. Metaphorically, it is the ability to synchronize life's beat to the rhythm of a calm breath and a heart full of love playing all elements in perfect equilibrium.
Vyakaranam	It is the analysis of grammar; composition of words, tenses, verbs; expansion of linguistic ability and discrimination. Metaphorically, it means to lead a life full of discrimination and to speak with purity and love.
Nirukta	It is an etymological account of difficult Vedic words. Metaphorically, it is an interpretation of the scriptures as a guide for the cultivation of soul consciousness.
Jyotisha	It means 'astrology,' 'light,' 'luster,' 'brightness,' 'flash,' and 'the light derived from the divine

	principle.' Metaphorically, it is to experience inner light through meditation, and to radiate the light of love and knowledge in every thought, word, and deed.
Kalpa	It is the set of prescribed rules laid down at rituals or ceremonies. Metaphorically, it means to perceive God in every thought.

The four remaining steps are Mimamsa, Nyaya, Dharmashastra, and the Puranas.

Mimamsa is 'deep reflection,' 'enquiry,' and 'philosophy.' The 'path of enquiry' is divided into two groups; Purva Mimamsa of Jainini and Uttara Mimamsa of Vyasa. Purva Mimamsa is an elaborate explanation and instruction on spiritual practices aiming at self-discipline and inner purification. Vyasa's Uttara Mimamsa is also known as Brahmasutra or Aphorisms on the Absolute Brahman, or even more famously, as Vedanta.

Nyaya is associated with Sage Goutama and is translated as 'Law' or 'The Science of Logic.' Metaphorically, it means to follow the path of justice, morality, and truth.

Dharmashastra is the Code of Law or Jurisprudence. In Sanskrit it is known as *smruti*. Metaphorically, *smruti* means 'memory' — to remember God in every breath. When there is a situation of confusion or conflict these *vidyas* are designed to show 'the right path.' The following sixteen *smrutis* are perhaps the most important: *manu smruti, yama smruti, vasistha smruti, atri smruti, vishnu smruti, angirasa smruti, usana smruti, vakpati smruti, vyasa smruti, apastamba smruti, goutama smruti, katyayana smruti, yajnavalka smruti, narada smruti, parasara smruti, samkha smruti.*

Puranas are part of an ancient encyclopedia containing various branches of knowledge, which form the backbone of Hindu Mythology. *Puran nava iti* is defined in the following way: while ancient, the message is still new (relevant). The Puranas, composed by Sage Vyasa, deliberate on five topics: *sarga* (creation), *pratisarga* (dissolution and recreation), *vamsa* (dynasty and genealogy), *manvantara* (the span and rule of the fourteen Manus), and *vamsacharita* (the story of each dynasty, especially the Solar and Lunar dynasties). The Puranas also include three of the most well-known scriptures; the Bhagavatam, the Ramayana, and the Mahabharata. Metaphorically, Puranas mean 'the indwelling Self;' 'the ancient One' or *purana/puratana.*

These are the fourteen disciplines (*vidyas*) needed to attain knowledge. In spiritual practice these fourteen represent the fourteen steps of breath up and down the seven chakras in the spine, while immersed in a state of deep meditation and communion with God. The purpose of knowledge is to realize the divine nature of the inner Self; whose essence permeates the entire universe.

Verse 6

tāvad vijñā bhavet sarvā
yāvad jñānaṃ na jāyate
brahmajñānaṃ padaṃ jñātvā
sarva vidyā sthirā bhavet

Translation

In spite of knowing all the above, one does not get knowledge of the Ultimate. Only by attaining *brahmajñana* (is) all other knowledge firmly established.

Metaphorical Interpretation

The path of knowledge is the path of liberation. True knowledge is awareness of the Self; which begins with the enquiry of 'Who am I?' and culminates with the experience of 'I am That.' This inner journey starts in the exterior world, controlled by the mind and the sense organs, and ends when the state of wisdom is attained through complete God-consciousness. Wisdom, in Sanskrit, is known as *prajña* or *prajñana.*

There are three stages to achieve the state of wisdom. The first stage is the 'acquisition of knowledge' or *jñana.* This encompasses the accumulation of theoretical knowledge received from different teachers and careful study of the scriptures.

The second stage is 'applied knowledge' or *vijñana.* This is the direct implementation of theoretical knowledge obtained from diverse sources, for the purpose of Self unfoldment. Once this is achieved, it is crucial to remain in a state of inner awakening, living a life of soul consciousness. The third and last stage is to be firmly established in a permanent state of wisdom *(prajñana).* When this summit is attained, a spiritual seeker becomes enlightened.

Every individual is blessed with four inner instruments comprising the mind, intellect, ego, and memory. Ordinarily, human intelligence is only used for material gain, yet life will remain incomplete unless it is filled with a spiritual component. In order to attain lasting and enduring happiness, a spiritual seeker must have a balanced development in the physical, emotional, mental, and spiritual spheres. Every living being needs food to survive but if the food is not easily digested or assimilated, even the most nourishing food can become a health hazard. Knowledge is the nutrition human beings require for a richer lifestyle but it must be assimilated, integrated, and applied in daily life. Book knowledge is indirect and therefore limited, Self-knowledge, on the other hand, is inexhaustable and can only be obtained through direct experience of Truth. Once the state of *shtitaprajna* is reached, a seeker becomes established in wisdom (Gita 2:54–68).

In this verse, Lord Shiva uses the words:

Padam jnatva 'knowing the feet' i.e., to attain divine knowledge, the Feet of God must be perceived inside the mind. A Vedic mantra illustrates this concept well, *tad vishno param padam*: "Those who are self-disciplined, the real heroes, will experience the Feet of the Supreme within the calmness of the mind, in the center of the third eye."

Sarva vidya encompasses all branches of knowledge. One of the Upanishads describes the Absolute as, *yasmin vijnate sarvam idam vijnanam bhavati*: "Having known the One, everything (else) is known." When real knowledge is grasped and assimilated, it automatically applies to every situation. A Self-realized person experiences God in all. A second meaning of *sarva vidya* refers to *dasa mahavidya,* the worship of the Divine Mother in all her different ten manifestations. This is in turn correlated with the ten incarnations of Vishnu, one aspect of the Hindu trilogy.

Sthira bhavet — when a person reads an inspiring work full of elevating thoughts or listens to a spiritual lecture, one transcends a mundane perspective, acquiring a glimpse of the inner Self for a short-lived moment. Nevertheless, a really spiritual person should constantly remain established in wisdom, experiencing Truth in every thought, word, and action. Just as a student who wishes to become a doctor must go to a medical school, a spiritual seeker must practice and imbibe all knowledge to achieve absolute proficiency as a yogi. Practice and discipline are the keys to success in life, both in worldly and spiritual terms.

Verse 7

veda śāstra purāṇāni
sāmānya gaṇikā iva
yā punaḥ śāmbhavī vidyā
guptā kula-vadhūriva

Translation

The Vedas, Shastras, and Puranas are like common entertainers compared to the *shambhavi vidya* — knowledge descending from Shiva — as the chaste lady of a noble family.

Metaphorical Interpretation

This passage indicates that acquisition of scriptural knowledge is available to all but is sometimes used for self-serving material advantage, fame, and fortune. Lahiri Mahashaya, a highly accomplished yogi, used to say, "Many talk about the scriptures, but only a rare few put them into practice," underlining the superficial scriptural knowledge devoid of practical application in everyday living.

Shambhavi vidya

Since scriptural knowledge is theoretical, it provides only temporary pleasure, but Self-knowledge or *shambhavi vidya* is the fountainhead of eternal joy. Self-realization has no identifiable external signs but manifests inwardly as divine peace, bliss, and joy. A common singer or entertainer may have temporary joy, may be won by flattery or money. But a chaste accomplished woman finds inner value and is like a hidden treasure of solid Self-knowledge. She is a source of bliss and freedom forever.

Shambhavi vidya is the accumulated wisdom of Shiva, attained through deep meditation. Shiva is the Supreme Yogi, constantly absorbed in meditation and unaffected by the disturbances and commotions of everyday life.

The essence of the Vedic scriptures is open *(mukta)* and at the same time concealed *(gupta)*. The hidden message is experienced only through inner awakening. The scriptures, as such, are available to everyone, but Truth, just like chastity, is a rare gift.

Verse 8

dehasthāḥ sarva vidyāśca
dehasthāḥ sarva devatāh
dehasthāḥ sarva tīrthāṇi
guru vākyeṇa labhyate

Translation

In this body can be found all the branches of knowledge, every god and goddess, and all the holy places, which can be reached only through the teachings of the guru.

Metaphorical Interpretation

Each body is a temple in which the soul manifests itself. It is a God-built shrine and should be treated with the dignity it deserves as a repository of divinity. A body should be taken care of through proper nourishment, cleansing, exercise, and rest. It is the building stone for spiritual evolution.

Sarva vidya

God and the entire divine creation reside within each being. Every individual contains a storehouse of all-encompassing wisdom but only a selected few can tap into the enormous energy hidden under the surface. *Vidya,* in this context, represents knowledge but also refers to *dasamahavidya,* a special way of worshipping the Divine Mother, source of universal energy.

Sarva devata

All deities or *sarva devata,* are only manifestations of the Supreme One present in each human shrine. In order to progress on the spiritual path, seekers must be able to transform their outlook towards the body, discipline the mind, and confirm the divinity latent within. If the body is seen to be all-important, it will lead to body consciousness, which is a source of bondage. Conversely, if a body is neglected it will lead to sickness. The human body is the temple of God, it should not be condemned, only subdued for the ultimate goal of transformation, the realization of "I am That" — the soul beyond the body.

Sarva tirtha

One major aspect of Hindu practice is to go on a pilgrimage to attain spiritual merit and purify the body and mind. Holy places are often located on the bank of rivers; at the confluence of rivers; by the ocean side; or on a mountain. Similarly, in each human body there are special places, holy like the places of pilgrimage, where divinity is manifested. Lord Shiva teaches, *dehasthāḥ sarva tīrthāṇi*: "All the holy places are located in the body."

Many scriptures vividly describe *teertha* as the divine qualities that can be cultivated during a lifespan. One of them, for instance, is *kshama teertha* or the quality of forgiveness. Just as the body and mind get cleansed while taking a dip in the river or ocean in a holy place, the mind becomes purified when it is suffused with divine qualities.

In the last part of this verse — *guru vakyena labhyate* — Lord Shiva speaks of the most crucial turning point in spiritual life, which is the relationship with the guru. Everything is possible through the words or grace of the guru. In reality, spiritual wisdom or experience is not the monopoly of gurus but of the Supreme Guru or God.

Nevertheless, only the most worthy student is able to perceive and assimilate the practical instructions handed down from one's predestined guru. A sincere devotee should possess the following qualities:

1) *Viveka* (good judgement or discrimination) — to be able to distinguish between what is real and what is unreal, permanent, or temporary,

2) *Vairagya* (dispassion) — the cultivation of non-attachment,

3) *Shama damadi shatsampathi* (the six-fold spiritual treasures)

   i) *shama* — control over the restless mind,

   ii) *dama* — control over the sense organs,

   iii) *uparati* — indifferent outlook for worldly endeavours; love for spiritual evolution,

   iv) *sraddha* — faith in the the holy scriptures and the teachings of the guru,

   v) *titiksha* — forbearance, equal-balance in all states of life; non-reactionary attitude,

   vi) *samadhana* — maintenance of the state of harmony and balance,

4) *Mumukshuttva* (strong yearning for liberation and emancipation).

A disciple, endowed with all these qualities, is worthy of receiving the grace of the guru, as well as his practical guidance, in order to experience the highest spiritual truth, embodied in the realization of the Absolute.

Verse 9

adhyātma vidyāhi nṛṇām
saukhya maukṣa karī bhavet
dharma karma tathā japyam
etat sarvaṃ nivartate

Translation

Through *adhyatma vidya* (the experience of spiritual wisdom), a person can obtain both happiness and liberation. All other preliminaries like *dharma, karma, and japa* will not be of any interest, thereafter.

Metaphorical Interpretation

Human life manifests itself through knowledge and love. Knowledge, according to the Mundaka Upanishad, is of two types: *para* (supreme spiritual wisdom) and *apara* (material knowledge).

Adhyatma vidya

To fully appreciate the hidden value of spiritual wisdom or *adhyatma vidya,* one must first understood *vyavaharika vidya* or material knowledge. Material knowledge leads to a life dedicated to pleasure-seeking activities, guided by the sense organs. This type of existence might seem alluring in the beginning but leaves the extrovert person with the inexorable feeling of anguish and emptiness. On the other hand, the spiritual path is much harder, since it requires a high dose of sacrifice, negation, and self-control. But ultimately, spiritual wisdom is the source of permanent joy; making the mind and senses introvert while quickening inner growth. Few choose the subtle spiritual path over that of worldly comfort. Yet with a clear mind, a discriminative intellect, a rational outlook, and sincerity to gain *adhyatma vidya,* a person can achieve a state of constant happiness and liberation.

Sukha and moksha

Sukha (happiness) and *moksha* (liberation) need further elaboration. Lahiri Mahasaya teaches,

kha sabda ākāśa brahman
samīpa kha sukha dureṇa kha duhkha

Kha is 'the formless sky' or Brahman, while *sukha* means 'happiness.' The metaphorical meaning is that happiness is derived from being closer to the sky, or the formless stage of divine consciousness. Distance from God results in suffering. The seeker who meditates by raising energy from the *vishuddha chakra* (throat center), to the cave of the cranium or the abode of God, will experience indescribable inner happiness, achieving liberation or *moksha*. *Moksha* is derived from two words, *moha* (delusion) and *kshaya* (elimination), i.e., to reach the stage where all delusion is eliminated and freedom from bondage is achieved. In order to reach this highly advanced ecstatic state of joy and liberation, different disciplines must be followed: these are known as *dharma, karma,* and *japa*.

Dharma

The Sanskrit word dharma has been incorrectly translated by modern scholars to mean religion. But dharma is a word with multiple meanings such as 'Law,' 'moral virtues,' 'Duty,' 'Justice,' 'property,' 'morality,' 'character,' 'nature,' 'manner,' 'good company,' 'devotion,' and 'the soul.'

The literal meaning of dharma is derived form the root verb *dhr* i.e., 'to hold or uphold,' in this sense dharma is 'that which upholds life.' Every breath has the all-important role of upholding the life principle in the body; breath, therefore, can be considered a form of dharma, at the root of our existence. Through breath or dharma, life prevails in a person. In the absence of breath or dharma, there is no strength, no beauty, no vitality, a body is dead and useless. Once the breath becomes the equivalent of dharma, or 'the upholder of life,' it is easier to understand the role of karma.

Karma

Karma represents 'action,' 'performance of religious rituals,' and 'moral duty.' Breath is equivalent to dharma, so a seeker should strive, through direct action (karma), to control the breath. Breath mastery will promote self-mastery or self-control over the extrovert senses. Karma, in this context, becomes *prana karma*, i.e., 'self-regulation' or 'mastery over the breath.' As a result, the spiritual aspirant will struggle to gain rigid control over physical, emotional, and intellectual activities eliminating all negative propensities and achieving a state of calmness, peace, and balance.

Japa

Japa means, in most spiritual practices, 'to repeat or chant the name of God' or a 'holy word.' But when *japa* is linked to karma, the organ of speech is used for a higher purpose. As it was explained in the first part of this volume, *japa* can be of three types: audible, in soft whisper, or mental chanting. In the context of inner spiritual practice, *japa* is 'to be conscious that every breath is the manifestation of God's love,' therefore bringing renewed energy into the body. This exercise is called *ajapa–japa,* i.e., non-chanting chant. The acquisition of spiritual wisdom instills a new outlook in the life of a devotee; ordinary things become extraordinary as one becomes absorbed in the state of permanent joy and all-encompassing love.

When one achieves the highest state of spiritual experience bestowing unfading and transcendental bliss all other practices and temporary satisfaction go away, as the lights of twinkling stars disappear with the rising sun.

Verse 10

kāṣṭha madhye yathā vahni
puṣpe gandhaḥ payo 'mṛtam
deha madhye tathā devaḥ
punyaṃ pāpaṃ vivarjitam

Translation

Like kindling in a fire, like the fragrance of the flower, and like cream in the milk, God resides in a body devoid of virtue or sin.

Metaphorical Interpretation

The basis of all spiritual and philosophical inquiry is for the Self or *ko'ham*: 'Who am I?' This is the most fundamental question during one's life journey. When a seeker finds the answer, realization is experienced. A path that helps a spiritual aspirant to experience the reality of life is to understand the role of the body and the mind by controlling these two fundamental aspects of life. A teacher, rather than a written text, becomes a valuable guide, since an enlightened guru provides a map for student's progress on the road of Self-enquiry. Books can only offer general descriptions, with complex meanings that are difficult to decipher, whereas the predestined guru gives his blessings and personalized guidance.

The One, the Eternal Self, beyond the reach of the senses, can only be realized through deep meditation. While immersed in ecstatic contemplation a devotee is able to grasp the vision of the indwelling power of God. The following mantra reveals the omnipresence of God in everyday objects:

tileṣu tailam dadhanīva sarpiḥ
āpaḥ srotaḥ-svaraṇīṣu cāgniḥ
evam ātmā' tmani gṛhyate 'sau
satyenainam tapasā yo' nupaśyatī

(The Shvetashvatara Upanishad, 1:15)

"As oil in sesame seed, as butter in cream, as water in the river bed, as fire in kindling sticks, so is the Self realized in one's own soul, if one looks for God with truthfulness and austerity. The Self which is the root of Self-knowledge and austerity that pervades all things; as butter is contained in milk, so is the Brahman, the highest mystical doctrine."

People offer oblations of *ghee* into the sacred fire. *Ghee* is made from milk, but if one pours milk into the fire, the fire will be extinguished. Yet, if butter is extracted from milk, by using a proper technique, and converted into *ghee* and subsequently offered to the sacred fire; it will enhance its brilliance. Similarly, although God is present in every individual, only through the path of self-discipline and meditation can inner Truth become manifested.

In this verse there are two words, *deha* or 'the body' and *deva* or 'God.' In Sanskrit, the body is called *deha* which consists of two parts, *de* and *ha*; the union of 'the formless' with 'form.' On the other hand, *deva* or God is the source of life, knowledge, and illumination.

Verse 11

īḍā bhagavati gaṅgā
pingalā yamunā nādī
īḍāpingalāyor madhye
suṣumnā ca sarasvatī

Translation

***Ida* is the divine river Ganga, *pingala* is the river Yamuna, and between *ida* and *pingala* lies *sushumna,* which is the Saraswati.**

Metaphorical Interpretation

Pilgrims travel a long way to visit holy places situated on the banks of rivers, or the mountaintops; or by the seashore. This involves physical strain, time, and energy. A truly spiritual seeker tries to find the 'holy places,' 'rivers,' and 'shrines' within one's inner universe.

In this verse, Lord Shiva mentions the main rivers present within the microcosm of the human body. Just as a river originates from the high mountains or lakes, and on its path other rivers join it, within the human body, there are numerous nerve-channels originating from the source of the cerebro-spinal system, with manifold veins and arteries, which carry not only blood, but in a symbolic way, the sum total of experiences, both physical and psychological, from one nerve plexus to another.

According to the Prashna Upanishad (3:6) there are 101 chief nerves, each again divided into 100 branches, and subject to further sub-division. In the scriptures there is an interesting parallel between some nerves (*nadis),* associated with specific parts of the human body, and which correspond, in turn, to the holy rivers of Bharata (ancient India).

NADI	**LOCATION**	**NAME OF THE RIVER**
Ida	from the left side of the brain to the *muladhara*	Ganga
Pingala	from the right side of the brain to the *muladhara*	Yamuna
Sushumna	the central channel inside the spinal cord	Saraswati
Kuhu	*muladhara* to *svadhisthana* (anus and genital area)	Narmada
Varuni	*svadhisthana* (genital organs)	Gomati
Payasvini	from the neck to the toes, in the right foot	Punpuna

Hastijihva	from the neck to the toes, in the left foot	Mahanadi
Pusa	the right eye	Tamraparni
Gandhari	the left eye	Kaveri
Yasasvini	the right ear	Godavari
Sankhini	from the left ear to the lower centers	Sarayu
Saraswati	the tip of the tongue	Brahmaputra
Visvadari	the belly	Tapti
Alambusa	the face	Goutami
Hastini	the nose	Sindhu

The cerebro-spinal system of a human being is a very intricate mechanism and remains a mystery, even to scientists, who are still trying to explore the source of infinite energy. This energy is manifested in the body through the spinal canal. In this verse, the three *nadis* (nerve-channels) *ida, pingala,* and *sushumna* are compared to the three holy rivers flowing inside the spine. *Merudanda* or the spine has a beautiful meaning: *meru* means 'the poles' such as the North Pole and the South Pole of the earth, and *danda* specifies 'a staff' or a 'vertical axis.' This is an illustration of the polarity in life being the root cause of boundless flowing energy.

Verse 12

triveṇī samgamo yatra
tīrtharāja sa ucyate
tatra snānamprakurvīta
sarva pāpairpramucyate

Translation

Where there is *triveni sangama* (the confluence of the three holy rivers), it becomes the holiest of holy places and by taking a bath there, one is freed from all sins.

Metaphorical Interpretation

Triveni stands for the confluence of the Ganga, the Yamuna, and the Saraswati, the place where the three holy rivers meet. This union is also known as *prayaga raj* or the 'royal confluence.' There are several *prayagas* (confluences) in the Himalayas, such as *rudra prayaga, karna prayaga, deva prayaga,* which are meeting points of these holy rivers. Since time immemorial, saints, sages, and countless spiritual aspirants have been living and meditating at such places. A good example is the holy city of Allahabad, the site of the historic Kumbhamela, every twelve years.

Teertha in Sanskrit has multiple meanings such as: 'passage,' 'road,' 'a way,' 'a descent into the river,' 'a place of water,' 'a holy place,' or 'a sacred teacher.' *Teertharaja* signifies 'the most holy place.' That taking bath or a dip in a holy river purifies one of sins and helps attain liberation is one of the major beliefs in Hindu tradition. Therefore, *teertha* also means a place of pilgrimage.

In the previous verse we discussed how the inner rivers are in reality energy channels within the body. The *ajna chakra* and the *muladhara chakra* correspond to the two major places of confluence where the *ida* (Ganga), *pingala* (Yamuna), and *sushumna* (Saraswati) meet. The upper junction, *ajna chakra* is known as *yukta triveni* or 'united confluence.' The lower junction is called *mukta triveni* or 'separated confluence,' located at the base of the spine; it is the playground of instincts and emotions. A true seeker must raise consciousness to the upper confluence to experience inner peace, bliss, and joy.

Papa in Sanskrit is 'sin.' But what is really sin? The greatest sin is to forget, "Who am I?" and to think, "I am the body." To commit repeated mistakes, through the senses, is a sin. *Sarva* means 'all,' but it can also mean 'the senses.' *Sarvapapa* is to cultivate a pleasure-seeking attitude in life. How to be free from this? The answer is to take a cleansing bath and regain inner purity. A body can be cleansed externally with water, but that is not the true meaning; the holy scriptures advocate, *snanamana malatyaga*: "A bath is the purification of the mind." To be free from all negative tendencies and impurities, a devotee should come up to the place of knowledge, i.e., *ajna chakra* and become immersed in soul consciousness. In this holy sanctum, a spiritual aspirant is purified and freed from the sinful clutch of the senses.

Verse 13

kīdṛśī khecari mudrā
vidyā ca śāmbhavī punah
kīdṛśyādhyātma vidyā ca
tanme brūhi maheśvara

Translation

Devi asked, "O Maheshwara, please explain to me what is *khechari mudra*, what is *shambhavi vidya,* and what is the meaning of *adhyatma vidya.*"

Metaphorical Interpretation

In this verse, Parvati, the Divine Mother, asks three questions:

1) What is *khechari mudra?*
2) What is *shambhavi vidya?*
3) What is *adhyatma vidya?*

Khechari mudra

Khechari mudra is a yogic practice, described in many traditional and classical texts and scriptures. In Hatha Yoga it is defined as the elongation and penetration of the tongue into the upper passage of air, or the epiglottis.

In the Shiva Samhita (Verses 53–54), *khechari mudra* is glorified in the following terms,

mudraisa khecari proktā bhaktānāṃ anurodhatah
siddhināṃ jananī hyeṣa mama prāṇādhikādhike priye
nirantara kṛtābhyāsam pīyuṣaṃ pratyahaṃ pibet
tena nigrahaṃ siddhisyāt mṛtyu matanga kesari

"At the request of the devotees, *khechari mudra* is revealed; it is the mother of all success, and even dearer than my own life. Practice it continuously, and drink the divine nectar daily. In this way, one gets the state of inner peace, similar to the one that ensues at the end of a war between the elephant and the lion, resulting in the death of the elephant."

Allegorically this means bringing thorough control over the breath and desires.

Shambhavi vidya

Shambhavi vidya is also a yogic practice of meditation. The name itself is derived from Shambhu, a synonym for Shiva. Shambhu signifies *samyak - bhu* or 'perfect manifestation.' In classical yogic literature it is accurately described,

antar lakṣa bahir dṛṣti nimeṣa unmeṣa varjitā
mudrā tu śambhavī proktā sarva tantreṣu gopitā

"Inner goal and outer look, without blinking of the eyes is *shambhavi mudra,* a hidden secret technique described in most Tantras."

Adhyatma vidya

Vidya comes from the root verb *vid,* which means 'to know,' so *vidya* is the equivalent of knowledge. The Mundaka Upanishad declares that *vidya* or knowledge is of two types, *para* or 'supreme knowledge' and *apara* or 'relative knowledge' of the material world. Real knowledge is Self-knowledge, otherwise known as *adhyatma vidya*. The Bhagavad Gita (10:32) describes *adhyatma vidya* or 'spiritual knowledge' as the best form of knowledge. Through simple living, positive thinking, a lifestyle devoid of ego, and the daily practice of meditation, a seeker acquires spiritual knowledge, experiencing inner bliss and peace. Lord Shiva elaborates further on these three topics in the following verses.

Verse 14

īśvara uvāca
manaḥ sthiraṃ yasya vināvalambanam
vāyu sthiro yasya vināvarodhanam
dṛṣṭiḥ sthirā yasya vināvalokanam
sā eva mudrā vicaranti khecari

Translation

Ishwara said, "The state where the mind is steady, independent of any support, where *vayu* (the breath) is tranquil and effortless, and where the gaze is still, without perception, is *khechari mudra*."

Metaphorical Interpretation

Restlessness is a symbol of activity while calmness leads to liberation. To live in the world successfully is to master the art of inner stillness. To be calmly active and actively calm is taught by all the great spiritual masters. Every spiritual path underlines the paramount importance of attaining the state of calmness. In this verse, Lord Shiva concentrates on the three stages of stillness that need to be cultivated in order to achieve spiritual progress:

i) Stillness of the mind,

ii) Stillness of the breath,

iii) Stillness in look and outlook.

Thorough control of the body, the mind and the breath are necessary tools for spiritual evolution. Like any other instruments, the body and the mind need to be kept healthy and strong. The body should be well toned, free from unnecessary fat or cumbersome folds of flesh. A body requires good hygiene, a proper diet, and adequate physical exercise on a daily basis.

The body and mind are correlated, so the mind must be kept calm, peaceful, and in strict control of the senses. A healthy mind is a strong mind, devoid of illusions. Proper attention should be given to the breath. Breath-control leads to mind-control. Yoga offers countless scientific techniques to achieve this.

If a person attains a calm and tranquil state, it is reflected in one's gaze, and inner composure. A quivering gaze is a symptom of a restless mind and an agitated lifestyle. A spiritual aspirant's look and outlook should be one of compassion and love, while being able to withdraw attention inwards and remain fixed in constant communion with the Absolute.

Verse 15

īśvara uvāca

bālasya mūrkhasya yathaiva cetah
svapnena hīno'pi karoti nidrām
tato gataḥ patho nirāvalambah
sā eva vidyā vicaranti śambhavi

Translation

Similar to the awareness of an innocent child or a naive person, or the awareness of deep dreamless sleep, proceeding in the path of meditation, without assistance, is called *shambhavi vidya.*

Metaphorical Interpretation

This verse explains the principle of *shambhavi vidya*, otherwise known as *shambhavi mudra*. The meaning of *shambhavi* is manifold: it is a synonym for Parvati; a way to describe green *durva* (a special grass used in Hindu rituals); a name used to portray the opening in the crown of the head through which the soul is said to escape once it leaves the body; and finally it is the name of a *yogic mudra* – a yogic practice.

Shambhavi mudra

Shambhavi mudra is one of the most complex forms of meditation. As described in Verse 13, it is "inner goal and outer look, without blinking of the eyes." A devotee must practice open-eyed meditation with attention fixed on the fontanel. The eyes must remain sightless and unblinking.

The Gheranda Samhita, a classical treatise on Yoga, speaks of *shambhavi mudra* in the following terms,

satyaṃ satyaṃ punaḥ satyam
satyaṃ ukta maheśvarah
śāmbhavi yo vijanīyāt
sa ca brahma jagannātha
(verse 3:67)

It is the truth repeatedly asserted by Lord Shiva, that one who knows and masters *shambhavi* is none but Brahman or Jagannatha, the Lord of the universe. With the practice of *shambhavi mudra*, meditation becomes more spontaneous, and devotees are able to experience the state of inner calmness and love, even with eyes wide open. When disciples perfect the practice of *shambhavi mudra*, they perceive all with childlike simplicity, the mind becomes free from agitation, and sleepless form of calmness will prevail, even while performing worldly activities.

Verse 16

devī uvāca
deva-deva jagannātha
brūhi me parameśvara
darśanāni kathaṃ deva
bhavanti ca pṛthak pṛthak

Translation

Devi asked, "O Lord of gods and Lord of universe, please tell me, O Parameshvara, what are the different *darshanas* (paths) for gaining experience?"

Metaphorical Interpretation

Devi (Parvati) asks Shiva, who is both her teacher as well as her companion, about the different ways of obtaining experience or realization. She addresses her husband as Deva-deva (Lord of gods), Jagannatha (Lord of the universe), and Parameshvara (Supreme Lord).

Deva comes from the root word *div,* which can mean 'vast as space' or 'self-luminous.' One, who experiences the formless stage and is always in the state of illumination, is Devendra, literally meaning 'Lord of gods.'

Jagannatha is a combination of two words, *jagat* 'that which changes continuously,' meaning 'the universe outside' and *nath* is 'Lord of all changes,' meaning the 'Changeless One.' Jagannatha is therefore known as 'Lord of the universe.' Whatever is perceived or experienced is the mixture of the two — the changing and the changeless — both are nothing but the manifestation of 'the One,' Parameshvara or the Supreme Lord.

In this verse, Parvati enquires about the different branches of *darshana,* i.e., philosophy. *Darshana* comes from the root verb *drs* which means 'seeing,' 'viewing,' and 'experiencing.' Thus, philosophy becomes the path of direct experience. Different levels of experience are gained as the embodied soul ascends on the spiritual path. In the following two verses, there is a description of the six schools of philosophical thought.

Verse 17

īśvara uvāca
tridanḍīca bhaved bhakto
vedābhyāsarataḥ sadā
prakṛti vādaratāḥ śāktāh
bauddhāḥ śūnyātivādinah

Translation

Ishwara said, "There are *tridandis* who are *bhaktas,* those on the path of knowledge who study and practice the Vedas, *shaktas* who worship nature, and *bauddhas* who are in favour of *shunyavada* (nothingness)."

Metaphorical Interpretation

In this verse, Lord Shiva speaks of four schools of Philosophy:

1) The Path of Devotion,
2) The Path of Knowledge,
3) The Path of Action,
4) The Path of the Nihilists.

Every individual has three basic types of character, integrated into their being, in varying proportions:

i) emotional heart,
ii) rational head,
iii) active hands.

The Path of Devotion

In this path emotion predominates, but when it becomes sublimated towards God or attaining a higher purpose in life, emotion becomes devotion. Lord Shiva describes a devotee on the Path of Devotion as a *tridandi.* The concept of *tridandi* is a technical one, since *tri* means 'three' and *danda* means 'self-discipline,' 'punishment,' 'stick,' or 'staff.' *Tridandi,* therefore, has several implications:

i) A spiritual mendicant,
ii) A person who has command over body, mind, and speech,
iii) A renunciate monk who holds three long staffs tied together. The three staffs are made of bamboo, bilva or aegle marmelos, and *asvatha* or Indian peepal,
iv) An evolved yogi who acquires control over the spine and the inner three channels: *ida, pingala, and sushumna.* The Path of Devotion requires discipline and self-control to enable the seeker to elevate emotion to the height of devotion.

In a classical yogic text, the Dattatreya Prokta Yoga Rahasya (verse 22), the concept of *tridandi* is explained in the following way,

vākdanḍaḥ karmadanḍaśca manodanḍaśca tritayā
yasaite niyatadanḍaḥ sa tridanḍi mahāyatih

"Disciplining speech, action, and mind is the path of self-discipline. One who has achieved this state is a great renunciate, and is called *tridandi* or holder of the three staffs."

The Path of Knowledge

Lord Shiva describes a devotee who follows this path as *vedabhyasaratah sada,* 'one who studies the scriptures integrating the teachings into daily life.' The Vedas are a means for translating spiritual knowledge into *abhyasa* or 'practice.' Knowledge alone leads to an increase of ego, but when it is put into practice, by leading a life according to the scriptures, it brings forth the true spirit of humility.

The Path of Action

Lord Shiva refers to *shaktas* as worshippers of the Divine Mother, the source of energy, strength, or ability. This path consists of worship, rituals, and direct involvement regarding nature. It also includes charity; serving the sick and the poor. In this way a seeker becomes free from ego and pride.

The Path of the Nihilists

In this path, Lord Shiva alludes to the Buddhists, or the followers of Buddha, who believe in *shunya vada* or that 'nothingness' leads to the state of final emancipation or enlightenment.

Verse 18

atordhaṃ gāmino yevā
tattvajña api tādṛsāh
sarvaṃ nāstīti cārvākāh
jalpanti viṣayāśritāh

Translation

There are also some who are always trying to go beyond everything, known as *tattvajnas* (who discriminate between the seen and the unseen) and some others called *charvakas,* who believe that nothing exists except enjoyment of the senses and who practice *jalpa,* being engrossed in *vishayas* (material enjoyment).

Metaphorical Interpretation

After describing the first four schools of philosophical thought, Lord Shiva elaborates on the remaining two branches:

5) The Path of the Realized,
6) The Path of Materialism.

The Path of the Realized

Every spiritual seeker strives to surpass all worldly limitations and go beyond the state of duality, full of conflict, bondage, and suffering in order to achieve final unity and experience liberation. A *tattvajna* (realized person) has experienced Truth and lives beyond all narrowness; having transcended the body, mind, ego, and intellect, completely saturated in a state of divine love.

The Path of Materialism

Lord Shiva speaks of a system of Philosophy enunciated by a sophistical philosopher known as Charvaka, believed to be the pupil of Brihaspati, who was known as the father of Atheism and Materialism. The primary meaning of Charvaka is 'one who speaks beautifully.' A Charvaka, in this context, is a person who appreciates the life of enjoyment and lives immersed in worldly pleasures offered by the material universe.

Verse 19

umā pṛcchati he deva
piṇḍa bramāṇḍa lakṣaṇam
pañca bhūta katham deva
guṇāḥ ke pañcaviṁśati

Translation

Then Uma (Parvati) asked, "O Lord, what are the qualities of the body — microcosm and the universe — macrocosm? What are the *panchabhutas* (five elements) and the twenty five *gunas* (qualities)?"

Metaphorical Interpretation

Uma is a synonym of Parvati, literally meaning 'the Divine Mother who is always interested in the acquisition of knowledge.' The dialogue between Shiva and Parvati is a constant theme within tantric texts. Here Parvati asks three fundamental questions:

i) What is the nature of the body (microcosm) and the universe (macrocosm)?
ii) What are the five elements?
iii) What are the twenty-five *gunas* (qualities)?

These enquiries are related to the physical body as well as the creation of the inner and the outer universe. In the same way that the body is the playground of the soul, the universe is the playground of the Absolute. In this context, *pinda* means 'the body' but literally, *pinda* means 'a morsel of food offered at death rituals' or 'during the anniversary of a departed soul.' *Pinda* can also mean a 'fetus' or 'embryo.' *Brahmanda* indicates 'the egg of Brahman,' or the primordial state from which the universe springs. *Lakshanam* is 'a distinctive trait,' 'characteristic,' or 'indication.' Parvati asks Shiva for further elaboration of the inner and the outer universe; the microcosm and the macrocosm, made of the five elements, i.e., earth, water, fire, air, and space in conjunction with twenty-five qualities.

Verse 20

īśvara uvāca
asthi māmsa nakhaṃ caiva
tvak lomāni ca pancamam
pṛthvi pañca guṇāḥ poktā
brahmajñānena bhāṣate

Translation

Ishwara said, "Those who have knowledge of Brahman (spiritual knowledge) say, bones, flesh, nails, skin, and hair constitute the five *gunas* (qualities) of the earth element."

Metaphorical Interpretation

Knowledge is not only a subject matter for discussion and debate but it is, above all, the state of freedom from doubts, confusion, and conflict. Self-knowledge, or *brahmajñana,* is the highest form of knowledge, bringing complete freedom to the enlightened individual in spite of living in a body composed of elements, and in a world full of duality. Those who meditate and contemplate on the subtle truth of life get the experience of Reality and Truth.

Answering the questions raised in the previous verse, Lord Shiva explains the five qualities of the earth element predominant in the body, which consist of bones, flesh, nails, skin, and hair.

Asthi literally means 'bone,' metaphorically *a* means 'negation' and *sthi* means 'sustenance,' i.e., the skeleton is the substructure of the body but it has no value without the presence of the soul. While the bones are an essential component, they are still impermanent.

Mamsa literally means 'flesh' but the metaphorical interpretation recalls the presence of divinity (*ma-amsa)*, since all that is manifested is none but God.

Nakha means 'nails,' but in allegorical terms *na* is 'not' and *kha* is 'vast' or 'formless,' so *nakha* is 'that which sets a limit.'

Tvak is 'skin,' but if the word is taken apart, *tu* means 'indeed' and *aka* means 'negative quality,' so *tu* + *aka* metaphorically indicates a place where negative qualities reside. The skin, overloaded with sensory perception and the constant lure for pleasure, becomes a great obstacle on the road to spiritual evolution.

Loma literally means 'hair.' The human body is covered with hair except for the palms and the lower part of the feet. Hair, symbolically, represents the last state of creation — *la* + *om; la* is derived from *laya* or 'cessation' and *om* means 'the state of creation.'

Verse 21

śukra śoṇita majjā ca
mala mūraṃ ca pañcamam
apāṃ pañca guṇāḥ proktā
brahma jñānena bhāṣate

Translation

Those who have the knowledge of Brahman say, semen, blood, marrow, stool, and urine are the five *gunas* of water.

Metaphorical Interpretation

In this verse, Lord Shiva elaborates on the five qualities of the water element. Approximately three-fourths of the earth is composed of water and the same proportion applies to the human body. When the water element is associated with the gross body, five visible qualities are manifested: semen, blood, marrow, stool, and urine.

Sukra stands for 'purity' and 'clarity' but in its role as 'semen' it is also interpreted as 'strength' and 'vitality.' Just as water cleanses and purifies the body, the semen, indispensable fertilizer, is an active principle in maintaining God's creation.

Shonita literally means 'blood' but symbolically it signifies 'activity,' which is a *rajasic* quality. Through an efficient circulatory system, a human being is able to accomplish numerous physical and mental activities; blood is not only associated with the heart or the brain but is also essential in the digestive process.

Majja, simply means 'marrow.' Just as the marrow is the innermost part of the bone, from which everything is derived, *majja* is the essence of divinity from which everything is manifested; *mat* + *ja* —'from Me everything is born.'

Mala could mean 'excreta' or 'impurity,' but it also refers to *maya* or 'delusion.' Literally, *ma* means 'mind' and *la* means 'destruction.' The essential quality of the water element is the cleansing of all impurities.

Mutra is 'urine,' but metaphorically refers to the divine experience through pleasurable contemplation.

Verse 22

nidrā kṣudhā tṛṣṇā caiva
klantiḥ ālasya pañcakam
tejaḥ pañcaguṇāḥ proktā
brahma jñānena bhāṣate

Translation

Knowers of Brahman say, sleep, hunger, thirst, fatigue, and idleness are the five *gunas* or qualities of the fire element.

Metaphorical Interpretation

In this verse, Lord Shiva explains the five qualities of the fire element: sleep, hunger, thirst, fatigue, and laziness. Fire is the third element. The sun is the source of fire, and yet paradoxically, in the epicenter of the earth there is molten lava, symbolizing fire. Balance between the inner and outer fire brings about the manifestation of life, but if an imbalance exists, there are disastrous consequences.

Nidra	means 'sleep,' but symbolically it represents forgetfulness of the breath (God-consciousness), due to extreme activities.
Kshudha	is 'hunger,' but allegorically, it designates desire for spiritual wisdom.
Trishna	means 'thirst,' interpreted as thirst for evolution.
Klantih	stands for 'fatigue,' metaphorically it means 'attachment.'
Alasya	is 'laziness' or lack of interest in both the material and spiritual worlds. The fire element, in this context, becomes a weak, flickering flame.

Verse 23

dhāraṇaṃ cālanaṃ kṣepam
samkocaṃ prasaraṇaṃ tathā
vāyoḥ pañcaguṇāḥ proktā
brahma jñānena bhāṣate

Translation

Knowers of Brahman say, to hold, to move, to throw, to

contract, and to expand are the five *gunas* or qualities of the air element.

Metaphorical Interpretation

Air is essential in the external world to all living things just as *prana* (the breath) is the vital energy in the inner world. Air is one of the subtlest elements, comprising the following five qualities: 'to hold,' 'to move,' 'to throw,' 'to contract,' and 'to expand.'

Dharana is 'to hold' or 'to support.' Air, water, and temperature are indispensable elements but out of the three, air is the most vital aspect of life. The breath is the source of life. When breath stops, life itself comes to a halt. In spiritual life, through rhythmic breathing, a devotee can behold Truth.

Chalanam literally means 'to move.' The breath activates the body, in the same way that the wind blows. Breath sets the body in motion; likewise spiritual life can only be possible through breath-control.

Kshepam means 'to throw' or 'to project.' Just as a hurricane can uproot trees and damage houses; a strong breath, full of anger or excessive emotion can reap havoc in life. Every angry word coming out of the mouth becomes like a weapon, since we use air to speak. Every word has the potential to maintain or destroy peaceful harmony.

Samkocha means 'contraction,' 'withdrawal,' or 'shyness.' Contraction becomes possible due to the intake of air, similarly a devotee can withdraw all senses from restlessness and experience calmness through breath-control.

Prasarana is the principle of 'expansion.' Air expands with an increase of temperature. In the same way, life expands when it is filled with the warmth of love and self-reliance brought on by an increase of knowledge.

Verse 24

kāmaṃ krodhaṃ tathā moham
lajjā lobhaṃ ca pañcamam
nabhau pañcagunāḥ proktā
brahma jñānena bhāṣate

Translation

According to Brahmajnana, kama (desire), krodha (anger), moha (delusion), lajja (indolence), and lobha (greed) are the five gunas of the ether element.

Metaphorical Interpretation

In this verse, Lord Shiva explains the five qualities of the ether element: *kama* (desire), *krodha* (anger), *moha* (delusion), *lajja* (indolence), and *lobha* (greed). These are the inner vices innate to most human beings. Although they manifest in the lower centers of the spine, their place of origin stems from the heart, which is the fountainhead of all emotions.

Kama literally stands for 'lust,' 'wish,' 'desire,' 'affection,' and 'love for sensual enjoyment.' Metaphorically, *ka+a* means 'happiness' and *ama* means 'unripe.' Unripe or immature happiness is born out of sensual pleasure and subsequently brings pain, unhappiness, emptiness, and even disease.

Krodha is 'anger' or 'wrath.' Metaphorically, *k* is 'happiness' and *rodha* means 'to stop' or 'to obstruct.' *Krodha* is a state that obstructs true happiness, since anger fills life with pain and misery.

Moha means 'loss of consciousness,' 'perplexity,' 'delusion,' 'attachment.' It is a delusive state that prevents a person from discerning Truth.

Lajja can be interpreted as 'shyness,' 'indolence' or 'laziness.'

A slothful person is intrinsically inactive and lacks the necessary will-power or discipline to make any headway in both the material and spiritual worlds.

Lobha means 'covetousness,' 'avarice,' and 'greed.' This state of confusion brings on a permanent feeling of dissatisfaction.

Verse 25

ākaśāt jāyate vāyuḥ
vāyoḥ utpadyate raviḥ
raverutpadyate toyam
toyāt utpadyate mahī

Translation

Vayu (air) is born of akasha (sky), from the air, ravi (fire) is born, from the fire, toya (water) is born, and from the water, mahi (earth) is born.

Metaphorical Interpretation

This verse refers to the process of creation from the formless state of ether (space) to the solid state of earth. In the Taittiriya Upanishad (2:1:3), a similar description is given,

tasmād va etasmād ātmana ākāśaḥ sambhūtah
ākāśād vāyuḥ, vāyor agniḥ, agner āpaḥ, adbhyoḥ pṛthivī

"From this Self, verily arose ether, from ether air, from air fire, from fire water, from water earth, and so on."

The following chart correlates a particular element and its corresponding sense organ, illustrating the connection between the inner and outer universe.

ELEMENTS	PRINCIPLE	QUALITY AUXILIARY	QUALITY SENSE ORGANS
Ether/Sky	sound		ear and speech
Air	touch	sound	skin and hands
Fire	sight	touch and sound	eyes and feet
Water	taste	sight, touch, sound	tongue and genitals
Earth	smell	taste, sight, touch, and sound	nose and anus

Life's energy, charged with the power of God, descends from the *ajna chakra* (soul) to the *vishuddha chakra* (ether), and from there to the *anahata chakra* (air), then to the *manipura chakra* (fire), further down to the *svadhisthana chakra* (water), and ultimately to the *muladhara chakra* (earth).

Verse 26

mahī vilīyate toye
toyaṃ vilīyate ravau
ravirvilīyate vāyau
vāyurvilīyate tu khe

Translation

Earth dissolves into water, water into fire, fire merges into air and air into ether/sky.

Metaphorical Interpretation

At this stage, Lord Shiva speaks of the process of dissolution, which is the reverse of the process of creation. Metaphorically, a spiritual aspirant should lift consciousness from the *muladhara chakra* to the *ajna chakra* and ultimately, to the *sahasrara chakra* or the crown of the head. The five chakras in the spine represent the five *tattvas* — principles or elements. The *sahasrara chakra* is beyond *tattva* and is referred to as *tattvatita.*

Verse 27

pañcatattvāt bhavet sṛṣṭih
tattvāt tattve vilīyate
pañcatattvāt paramtattvam
tatvātīta nirañjanam

Translation

Creation manifested (Itself) from the above five elements. The *tattvas* merge into one another and above the five *tattvas* is *paramtattva* (Supreme Principle); *niranjana* (the Formless) is beyond the *tattvas.*

Metaphorical Interpretation

Any living creature or inanimate object has a physical body and is made of the five elements. The process of quintiplication is equivalent to the process of transformation from a subtler essence to a gross state.

Space	=	1/2space	+1/8th air	+1/8th fire	+1/8th water	+ 1/8th earth
Air	=	1/2air	+1/8th space	+1/8th fire	+1/8th water	+ 1/8th earth
Fire	=	1/2fire	+1/8th space	+1/8th air	+1/8th water	+ 1/8th earth
Water	=	1/2water	+1/8th space	+1/8th air	+1/8th fire	+ 1/8th earth
Earth	=	1/2earth	+1/8th space	+1/8th air	+1/8th fire	+ 1/8th water

Beyond these five *tattvas* (principles or elements) is the Supreme Principle, which is none but the Formless One, known as Brahman.

"When a seer sees the Creator of golden colour, the Lord, the source of Brahma, one becomes the knower, free from strain, shaking off good and evil and attaining the Supreme State."

Mundaka Upanishad (3:1:3)

Verse 28

sparśanaṃ rasanaṃ caiva
ghrāṇaṃ cakṣuśca śravanam
pañcendriyaṃ idaṃ tattvam
manaḥ sādhanyaṃ īndriyam

Translation

Touch, taste, smell, sight, and hearing are the five *indriyas* (organs of perception), which are the instruments of the mind.

Metaphorical Interpretation

In this verse, the five elements are correlated with the sense organs.

ELEMENTS	ORGANS OF PERCEPTION	ORGANS OF ACTION	OBJECTS
Ether	Ear	Mouth	Sound
Air	Skin	Hands	Touch
Fire	Eye	Feet	Sight
Water	Tongue	Genitals	Taste
Earth	Nose	Anus	Smell

The senses are the instruments of the mind, but the mind remains the controlling factor. In the Katha Upanishad (1:3:4), there is a description that the soul experiences the world, with the help of the mind and the senses. A well-balanced life requires a healthy mind, a discriminative intellect, and a balanced use of the five sense organs. The *devas* (presiding deities) are in attendance at each one of the sense organs (*indriya*). The presiding deity is *devaraja* (supreme *deva*), otherwise known as Indra (the ruler), who controls, guides, and directs the senses.

Verse 29

bramhāṇḍa lakṣaṇaṃ sarvam
dehamadhye vyavasthītam
sākāraśca vinaśyati
nirākāraṃ na naśyati

Translation

All the qualities of *Brahmanda* (macrocosm) are also present in the body. The form is perishable while what is formless does not perish.

Metaphorical Interpretation

Microcosm and macrocosm are one; just as the body and the universe are essentially one. The entire universe with its stars, planets, solar system(s), atmosphere, living beings, rivers, mountains, stones, and grains of sand is nothing but the sum total of the five elements: space, air, fire, water, and soil, imbued in an all-pervasive cosmic consciousness. The human body, or microcosm, is also composed of the same five elements.

One God who is all-pervading, remains in every living being as the embodied soul, *atman*. The universe is nothing but God alone and every individual is nothing but Brahman, the Formless Spirit. Every human body is a microcosm, a little universe. Both the universe, as well as the individual, share the same characteristics: *sakara* (form) and *nirakara* (formless). Each living being has a body with a form and a soul, which is formless. In the same way, the universe in its vastness has a complete form, while it remains permeated by the Cosmic Being, Brahman, or the Formless God.

A seeker, through sincere spiritual practice, can realize the Absolute and feel complete oneness with creation. This is the state of unity. Every yogi and sincere meditator has experienced Truth by introverting the senses and going within.

CREATION

Microcosm (Individual)	**Macrocosm (Universe)**
Body and Soul	Physical Existence (Form) and God (Formless)
Form	**Formless**
Is finite	Is infinite
Is born and must die	Is beyond birth and death (immortal)
Undergoes six modifications (growth,	Is beyond modificationmaturity)
Is able to experience through the five senses	Is transcendental
Is composed of the five elements	Is beyond the five elements

To understand form and formless, an appropriate analogy is of the gold in an ornament. Gold as such is formless, but under an able goldsmith it can assume many forms. The new forms are only a superimposition on the gold. When the form is removed and the ornament or coin is melted down, the gold goes back to its original state, becoming pure gold once again. In a similar manner, the body and the soul, as well as the universe and the Absolute, can be experienced and realized.

In the Shvetashvatara Upanishad (6:2 and 4) it is said,

> "He, by whom this whole world is always enveloped, the Knower, the author of time, the possessor of qualities and all knowledge. Controlled by Him, this work of creation unfolds itself; that which is regarded as earth, water, fire, air, and ether.
>
> Who, having begun with undertakings associated with the (three) qualities, distributes all existence. In the absence of these qualities, there is destruction of the work that has been done and in the destruction of the work, He continues."

Verse 30

nirākāraṃ mano yasya
nirākāra samo bhavet
tasmāt sarva prayatnena
sākāraṃ tu parityajet

Translation

One whose mind is fixed on the Formless becomes formless. Therefore through every effort, go beyond form.

Metaphorical Interpretation

In this verse, Lord Shiva underlines the importance of experience, through the instrument of the mind. A restless mind encounters movement, turbulence, and instability, within a constantly changing universe. A calm and tranquil mind is able to experience the changeless, immortal soul seated at the crown of the head (*sahasrara*). As is the mind, so is the person, and ultimately the experience.

Lord Shiva teaches that while performing all sincere endeavours, a devotee should try to go beyond form into formlessness, and thus reach union with the Absolute.

A great poet-philosopher and spiritual master of India, Swami Madhusudana Saraswati sang,

hari reva jagat jagadeko hari
harito jagato nahi bhinnatanu
iti yasya mati paramātma rati
sa naro bhava sāgara nistarati

"Hari alone is the universe and the universe alone is Hari; there is no difference between the universe and Hari. One who keeps the mind in such a state, with deep love for God, indeed crosses the ocean of the world."

Verse 31

devī uvāca
ādinātha mayi brūhi
saptadhātuḥ kathaṃ bhavet
ātmā caivāntarātmā ca
paramātmā kathaṃ bhavet

Translation

Devi asked, "O Adinatha (First Guru) please tell me what are the *saptadhatus* (seven ingredients or essences)? What is *atma* (soul)? What is *antaratma* (inner soul)? What is *paramatma* (Supreme Soul)?"

Metaphorical Interpretation

In this verse, Parvati or the Divine Mother has the following enquiries:

i) What is meant by *saptadhatu?*
ii) What is *atma?*
iii) What is *antaratma*?
iv) What is *paramatma*?

Adinatha means 'First Guru.' *Adi* symbolizes in the beginning; the time before creation. The implicit message is that Lord Shiva was there from the beginning; he is therefore omniscient and omnipotent, possessing direct knowledge of everything.

Verse 32

īśvara uvāca
śukra śoṇita majjā ca
medo māmsaṃ ca pañcamam
asthi tvak caiva saptaite
śarīreṣu vyavasthitāḥ

Translation

Ishwara said, "In the body the *saptadhatus* (seven constituents) are present, which are: semen, blood, marrow, fat, flesh, bones, and skin."

Metaphorical Interpretation

In this verse, Lord Shiva enumerates the *saptadhatus* or seven constituents: *sukra* (semen), *sonita* (blood), majja (marrow), *meda* (fat), *mamsa* (flesh), *asthi* (bone), and *tvak* (skin). In Ayurveda and other yogic scriptures, *rasa* (plasma /fluid) is mentioned instead of the skin.

The three-fold activities of the seven *dhatus* are:

NAME	BODILY EXCRETION	MAJOR ACTIVITY	MINOR ACTIVITY
Rasa	cough	Maintenance of Plasma	Supports kidney and spleen
Rakta	bile (*pitta*)	Colour pigment	Helps to nourish the skin
Mamsa	ear-wax	Maintains the skin	Nourishes fat
Meda	sweat	Nourishes fat	Helps the bone
Asthi	nail, hair	Nourishes the bone	Helps the marrow
Majja	tear	Nourishes marrow	Semen
Sukra	no impurity	Nourishes semen	*Ojah* (human magnetism)

This table explains the triple functions of the seven elementary substances in the body. Among the seven *dhatus*, the first six are feminine and the seventh is the masculine aspect.

Verse 33

śarīraṃ caivaṃ ātmānam
antarātmā manobhavet
paramātmāṃ bhavet śūnyam
mano yatra vilīyate

Translation

The soul in the body is *atma*, the mind is called *antaratma*, and *paramatma* is the formless state where mind is dissolved.

Metaphorical Interpretation

In addition to the explanation in Verse 31, the body is considered as the *atma,* the mind as the *antaratma,* and the state of formlessness as *paramatma*, where the mind becomes completely dissolved. But to accept the body as the Self or the soul seems inappropriate. The individual is not considered the soul but the embodied soul. In Sanskrit, *jiva* is the term used to refer to an embodied or individual soul.

Many persons take care of the external needs of the body, but only a very few really take care of the mind. The body and the mind both need exceptional care in order to cultivate a healthy lifestyle and true spirituality. In reality, *atma* is defined as *atate vyapnoti iti*: "That which is formless and immortal, with the attribute of pure consciousness and bliss." *Atma* or the individual soul and *paramatma* or the Supreme Soul (Brahman) are essentially one; like the waves in the ocean. To experience this state of absolute unity, the spiritual seeker needs the help of an inner instrument, the mind, called *antaratma* or literally 'the inner Self.' Mind is like a tool, which helps a person to evolve, but once the target is reached, it ceases to be useful and should dissolve. The experience of Truth is beyond the senses and the mind.

Verse 34

raktadhātu bhavet mātā
śukradhātu bhavet pitā
śunyadhātu bhavet prāṇo
garbhe piñḍaṃ prajāyate

Translation

Taking the *raktadhatu* (element of blood) from the mother, the *shukradhatu* (element of semen) from the father, and the *shunyadhatu* (vacuum) from the *prana* (vital air), the fetus forms in the womb.

Metaphorical Interpretation

This verse has various interpretations:

1) Traditionally, a woman's fertility is connected to the time of menstruation (changes in the nature of blood through the process of ovulation). The ovum of the mother and the sperm of the father unite in the space of the uterus to bring forth new life in the fetus or embryo, which is known as *pinda* in Sanskrit. This is the new abode for the itinerant soul.

2) *Rakta* means 'red,' 'crimson,' 'coloured,' 'attached to love,' or 'blood.'
Shukra means 'white,' 'bright,' 'radiant,' 'pure,' 'fire,' or 'semen.'
Shunya means 'empty,' 'void,' 'zero,' 'space,' 'atmosphere,' or 'Brahman.' All three are different stages of experience during meditation.

3) *Rakta* is related to the *rajasic* quality of the colour red.
Shukra is related to the *sattvic* quality of the colour white.
Shunya is related to the *tamasic* quality of the colour black.
These qualities together represent nature. The union of *prakriti* (nature) and Purusha (Shiva or the indwelling Spirit) is the cause

of all creation.

4) *Raktadhatu* stands for activity.
Shukradhatu is translated as 'purity,' which is nothing but the soul.
Shunyadhatu means life-energy.
The combination of these three elements can be interpreted to mean that purity or the soul, with the help of *prana,* manifests activity in life.

Verse 35

devī uvāca

kathaṃ utpadyate vācā
kathaṃ vācā vilīyate
vākyasya nirnayaṃ brūhi
paśyam-jñānaṃ udāhara

Translation

Devi asked, "How is speech born and where does it dissolve? Please elaborate on the principle of speech through which knowledge is gained."

Metaphorical Interpretation

Speech is the most powerful means of communication. In the Upanishads it is said, *vāk vai agni, vāk vai brahman*: "Talk is like fire, talk is also God."

In this verse, the Divine Mother asks about the origin and dissolution of speech, and enquires how speech can ignite knowledge.

Verse 36

īśvara uvāca
avyaktāt jāyate prāṇah
prāṇāt utpadyate manah
manasotpadyate vāco
mano vācā vilīyate

Translation

Ishwara said, "From *avyakta* (the un-manifest), *prana* (vital air) is born, which gives birth to *mana* (the mind), which in turn generates speech, expressed through *vakya* (words)."

Metaphorical Interpretation

The origin of speech has four steps: *avyakta* (the un-manifest), *prana* (vital air), *mana* (the mind), and *vakya* (words).

In both Yoga and Tantra, there are four stages of speech: *para, pasyanti, madhyama*, and *vaikhari*. The word, expressed with sound, is the last stage.

STAGES	MODE OF SPEECH	LOCATION	STATE OF EXPERIENCE
Avyakta	*Para*	*Sahasrara*	Divinity
Prana	*Pashyanti*	*Ajna*	Visualization
Vakya	*Vaikhari*	*Vishuddha*	Expression
Mana	*Madhyama*	*Anahata*	Feeling

Para is the imperishable inner light from where all thoughts originate. *Pashyanti* is the stage before communication when there is no distinction of sound as such; it resides in the vital breath. At this point, thoughts are perceived within. *Vaikhari* is manifested by the activity of the speech organ or the expression of sound. *Madhyama* remains present in *buddhi* (intellectual understanding), as it starts to make a distinction in the nature of sound but still dwells in the sphere of inner communication. It follows that the dissolution of speech takes place in the reverse order.

Lord Shiva emphasizes that from *avyakta* or the un-manifest, the vibration of *prana* or vital breath is generated, which becomes the source of the mind and ultimately of the thought process, which is expressed in words.

Verse 37

devī uvāca
kasmin sthāne vaset suryah
kasmin sthāne vaset śaśīh
kasmin sthāne vaset vāyuh
kasmin sthāne vaset manah

Translation

Devi asked, "Where is the abode of the sun, and where does the moon reside? Where does the vital air live, and what is the place of the mind?"

Metaphorical Interpretation

The Divine Mother enquires about the place of residence of *surya* or the sun, *sashi* or the moon, *vayu* or vital air, and *mana* or the mind.

Surya or the sun, is defined as *sarathi* or *akasha* — 'one who roams in space,' i.e., the experience of light in the inner sky.

yadva subati karmani lokam prerayati surya: "One who is the source of life and activities and motivates all living beings towards action is *surya*."

The sun is the presiding deity of the intellect and wisdom. Spiritual seekers chant the Gayatri Mantra to invoke spiritual wisdom within.

Sashi is one of the names given to the moon. There is a definition in Sanskrit that says, *saha asti anya iti* — the moon is the 'Lord of the mind.'

It is only through the mind and the intellect that a person can progress on the road to Self-evolution.

Vayu is the life breath or vital air. Yogis have identified fifty different types of breath.

Mana here represents the mind; life becomes the playground of the mind.

Verse 38

īśvara uvāca
tālu mūle sthitaḥ candro
nābhi mūle divākarah
sūryārgre vasate vāyuh
candrāgre vasate manah

Translation

Ishwara said, "The moon (*chandra*) is present at the base of the palate, and the sun (*surya*) is at the base of the navel. Above the sun is the vital air (*vayu*) and above the moon (*chandra),* is the mind."

Metaphorical Interpretation

In this verse, Lord Shiva answers the questions about the location of *surya, chandra (or sashi), vayu* and *mana,* in a technical manner,

Nabhi mule divakara — the sun or *surya* is at the root of the navel (*manipura chakra*). *Divakara* can be broken into two words, *diva* here means 'in the day,' *kara* is 'rays' or 'hands.' The metaphorical interpretation is 'that which brings all activities and life.' Above the place of the sun is the seat of *vayu/prana* or the vital air (*anahata chakra*).

Talumule sthito chandra — the moon or *chandra* resides at the root of the palate or uvula, near the *vishuddha chakra*. *Chandra* means 'glittering,' 'lovely.' A seeker, conscious of the mind, takes good care of it, makes it beautiful.

Above the moon is the place of the mind (*mana*) in the *ajna chakra*. When a yogi or a tantric practices *khechari mudra*, by bringing the tongue above the uvula, one attains all the qualities of the moon and the sun, by displaying control over the breath and the mind.

Mana (the mind)	*Ajna chakra* (soul center)
Chandra (the moon)	Below *Ajna chakra* up to *Vishuddha chakra* (cervical center)
Vayu (vital air)	*Anahata chakra* (dorsal center)
Surya (sun)	*Manipura chakra* (lumbar center)

Verse 39

sūryāgre vasate cittah
candrāgre jīvitam priye
etad yuktaṃ mahādevi
guruvākyeṇa labhyate

Translation

O Dear Parvati, *chitta* (memory) resides above *surya* (the sun) and the life principle is above *chandra* (the moon). All

these things are to be learned from the teachings of the guru (the divine master).

Metaphorical Interpretation

Since the sun is the Lord of the intellect, it is also the source of memory *(chitta)*. The faculty of memory is the retentive quality, which adds a special brilliance to the mind. To achieve this, inner attention must be fixed on the sun.

Chandragre jivitam — the moon is the source of *rasa* or 'the balancing and nourishing fluid within plants and animals.' In human beings, the life principle remains inside the brain, i. e., between the *ajna chakra,* and the *sahasrara chakra* or the crown of the head.

Lord Shiva emphasizes that all spiritual practices, concentration, and meditation, should be practiced under the instructions, guidance, and supervision of a qualified guru, but God remains the Supreme Master.

Verse 40

devī uvāca
kasmin sthāne vaset śaktih
kaśmin sthāne vaset śivah
kasmin sthąne vaset kālo
jarā kena prajāyate

Translation

Devi asked, "Which is the abode of *shakti* (divine energy), in which place does Shiva reside, which is the seat of *kala* (time/death), and where does *jara* (old age) come from?"

Metaphorical Interpretation

In this verse, the Divine Mother asks about *shakti, Shiva, kala,* and *jara. Shakti* is derived from the root verb *shak,* which means 'to be able to' or 'capable of.' So *shakti* or energy is translated as 'ability' or 'strength.' Strength is regarded with respect, but it is not limited to physical strength since it also encompasses mental, intellectual, and spiritual energy.

Shiva is *shava* (dead body) + *i* (the source of life and energy). *Shiva* is equivalent to the Soul, the source of all energy, life, and activities.

Kala is the 'time principle,' but it is also known as 'death.' Everything that is born must one day die. *Kala* is the flow of energy that is the cause of all projection and dissolution.

Jara comes from the verb *jar,* which means 'to become old.' Symbolically, *jara* is to grow and become mature, allowing weakness and emotion to die while becoming stronger through love and understanding.

Verse 41

īśvara uvāca
pātāle vasate śaktih
brahmāṇḍe vasate śivāh
antarīkṣe vaset kālo
jarā tena prajāyate

Translation

Ishwara said, "*Shakti* (divine energy) resides in *patala* (the nether region) and Shiva resides in *Brahmanda* (the universe). *Kala* is in *anthariksha* (the inner sky), from where *jara* (old age) is born."

Metaphorical Interpretation

In this verse, Lord Shiva points out the location of *shakti, Shiva, kala,* and *jara*.

The human body can be divided into three parts using the same terms for the universe:

patala	(the lower sphere of creation),
martya	(the earthly plane),
svarga	(the heavenly place).

The lower region, known as *patala,* is found from the hips downwards (there are seven *talas* or lower regions). From the hips upwards is the upper part with the seven *lokas* or worlds, which sub-divide into earthly and heavenly planes.

PLACE	PLANES OF EXISTENCE	INNER EXPERIENCES
Sahasrara (crown of the head)	*satyaloka*	Heavenly bliss
Ajna (third eye)	*tapoloka*	Intuition
Vishuddha (cervix)	*janaloka*	Intellect
Anahata (dorsal)	*maharloka*	Emotion/Earthly plane
Manipura (lumbar)	*svarloka*	Health
Svadhisthana (sacral)	*bhuvaloka*	Sexuality
Muladhara (coccyx)	*bhurloka*	Materialism
Hip	*atala*	Fear
Thighs	*vitala*	Anger
Knees	*sutala*	Jealousy
Calves	*talatala*	Greed/Deceit
Ankle	*rasatala*	Selfishness
Feet	*mahatala*	Blindness to one's own actions
Sole of the feet	*patala*	Destructive tendency/ Revenge

The Upanishads say, *padayoh shaktih*: "Strength resides in the feet." The feet symbolize movement; so a spiritual seeker is to proceed energetically forward. *Patala* is found at the sole of the feet, in the lowest of the seven planes of *talas*, it is from this region that *shakti* or energy rises to the higher planes. In reflexology, the entire human system is projected in the sole of the feet.

As has been described earlier in this text, the body's axis has polarity: while the *sahasrara* stands for the North Pole; the feet represent the South Pole. Therefore, the feet reflect energy the same way as the brain.

Shri Shankaracharya, in his prayer to Lord Shiva "Shiva Manasa Puja," exemplifies each human body as the temple of Shiva,

ātma tvaṃ girijā matiḥ sahacarāḥ prāṇāḥ śarira gṛiha ...

"O Lord Shiva, you are the Soul in me, my mind is Parvati and verily this body is your home, the temple. Every living being is described as Brahmanda or the residing place of Brahman. Shiva is inside every individual."

The term *antariksha* means 'space,' and refers to the space outside and inside the human body. Literally, *antariksha* is the intermediate region between heaven and earth. Metaphorically, in the human body heaven is the place from the *ajna chakra* to the *sahasrara,* while the earthly plane refers to the spine and the five lower chakras. *Kala* resides in the *antariksha,* close to the soul center, near the medulla oblongata. *Kala* (death) keeps measure of time. When time runs out, death comes.

Jara, or old age, is the product of deteriorated breath. *Jara* is also the name of a mythological demoness, who attempts to devour everyone.

One of the benefits of *mahamudra* (a yogic exercise) is described as, *jarā mṛityur vināśanam:* "The practice of *mahamudra* makes one free from the clutches of *kala* (death) and *jara* (old age)."

Verse 42

devī uvāca
āhāra kāñkṣate ko sau
bhuñjate pivate katham
jāgrat svapna suṣuptau ca
ko vā sau pratibuddhati

Translation

Devi asked, "Who is the one who needs food, how does one eat and drink, who is aware of the wakeful, dream, and deep sleep states?"

Metaphorical Interpretation

The Divine Mother enquires about the intake of food and nourishment for the body and the three stages of awareness of the spirit.

The word *ahara* derives from — *a-hriyate-iti* — meaning 'what one takes in' or 'consumes.' *Ahara* is therefore translated as 'food.' A human being consumes food for nourishment, but thoughts and ideas are also considered food for the mind. One experiences the world through the five senses of perception: sight, sound, touch, smell, and taste. Breath can also fit into the category of food, since we need to take in oxygen to survive. *Ahara,* interpreted in a broad sense, means that food is necessary for the body, the senses, and the mind.

Every day an individual passes through the three stages:

jagrata (the wakeful state); *svapna* (the dream state); and *sushupti* (the state of deep sleep).

Jagrata	(the wakeful state) — all three bodies, gross, astral, and causal are active and awake.
Svapna	(the dream state) — the gross body is at rest, but the astral and causal bodies are active.
Sushupti	(the deep sleep state) — in this state of ignorance only the causal body is active, the gross and astral bodies are asleep.

Verse 43

īśvara uvāca
āhāraṃ kāñkṣate prāṇo
bhunjate 'pi hutāśanaḥ
jāgrat svapna suṣuptau ca
vāyuśca pratibuddhati

Translation

Ishwara said, "*Prana* (the life force) needs food and eats and drinks through *hutasana* (the digestive fire). *Vayu* (the breath) is aware of the wakeful, dream, and deep sleep states."

Metaphorical Interpretation

In this verse Lord Shiva further elaborates on the question raised by Parvati:

Prani is a 'living being' — *pranam asti yasya sah* — means 'one who has the life-energy is a living entity.' Thus, *prani* encompasses humans, animals, and plants. Food, in some form, is essential to all living beings, only a dead entity, one without *prana* (the life-force) feels no hunger.

Hutasana is a name used for 'fire' consisting of two parts — *huta* and *asana,* i.e., 'the cry for food.' *Hutasana* is therefore a 'fire that creates a desire for food.' In the Gita (15:14), *vaisvanara* 'the digestive fire' is mentioned; this gastric fire becomes active due to the pranic energy functioning in the navel center.

Lord Shiva explains that at every stage of existence; breath is a necessity. Whether in the wakeful, dream, or deep sleep states, breath is the active and motivating force in every living being.

Verse 44

devī uvāca
ko vā karoti karmāṇi
ko vā lipyati pātakaih
ko vā karoti pāpāni
ko vā pāpaiḥ pramucyate

Translation

Devi asked, "Who is doing the action, who is committing mistakes, who is causing sinful acts and how are they redeemed?"

Metaphorical Interpretation

This question has elementary as well as subtle components. In this verse, the Divine Mother asks about karma, good and bad; *pataka*, *papa*, as well as how to be freed from *papa*.

Karma literally means 'action,' but in the context of the Hindu system karma refers to volitional activities, — physical, vocal, and mental — in words, deeds, and thoughts. The science of Physics maintains that each action has a potential result, so does karma. Each karma has an inevitable result. One needs to be watchful of one's action. Some consequences are immediate, others remain dormant and manifest in future lives.

Pataka is derived from the word *patana,* which means 'downfall'; *pataka* is therefore 'that action which brings downfall and disgrace to a person.' Literally, it is translated as 'a mistake' but sometimes the word is used to refer to something stronger, like 'sin.' In the Manu Smruti (11:54) it is said,

brahmahatyā surāpānam
steyam gurvānganāgamah
maḥānti pātakānyāhuh
samsargaççāpi taià saha

"To kill the wise, to drink alcohol, to steal, to enjoy or cohabit with the guru's wife, are (all) considered heinous activities. Even association with people who commit these (acts) is as deplorable as *pataka.*"

Papa means 'sin.' A mistake is committed out of ignorance, but if a mistake is repeated again and again, it becomes a sin. In essence, to forget the truth of life is a catalyst for mistakes, misery, and sin.

Verse 45

īśvara uvāca
manaḥ karoti pāpāni
mano lipyate pātakaiḥ
manaśca tanmayā bhūtvā
na puṇyaiḥ na ca pātakaiḥ

Translation

Ishwara said, "Mind commits mistakes and causes sinful acts. When the mind is in God-consciousness, it is free from virtue and vice."

Metaphorical Interpretation

Lord Shiva replies to all queries with one answer, "It is the mind." The mind is the cause of all activities, good or bad.

In the Amritabindu Upanishad (mantra 2) it is said,

mana eva manuṣyāṇām
kāraṇaṃ bandha mokṣayoh
bandhāya viṣayāsaktam
muktaṃ nirviṣayaṃ smṛtam

"Mind is the cause of bondage and mind is the cause of liberation. A mind engrossed in the material world is in bondage and a detached mind is in the state of liberation."

Every human being has three faculties: physical (body), psychological (mind), and spiritual (soul). The body dies but the soul remains ever pure. The mind can be dirty or clean; while a debased mind brings misery, a pure mind brings peace. All spiritual practices and spiritual disciplines are geared to obtain inner purity, calmness of the mind, and ultimately, liberation. When the mind is immersed in the state of divinity, it is beyond virtue and vice. In the state of liberation the mental components like virtue and vice become irrelevant. The word *tanmaya* is made up of *tat* or 'that' and *maya,* which here means 'saturation' or 'absorption,' i.e., 'a mind saturated in divine love.' Once the mind has reached this elevated state, it can only perceive Brahman.

Verse 46

devī uvāca
jīva kena prakārena
śiva bhavati kasya ca
kāryasya kāraṇaṃ brūhi
kathaṃ kiṃ ca prasādhanam

Translation

Devi asked, "How does *jiva* (the individual soul) become Shiva (the universal Soul)? Please explain what is the cause of action, which is the effect, and how is it accomplished?"

Metaphorical Interpretation

Parvati asks about *karya* (action), *karana* (cause), and the means to become realized. The very essence of spiritual life is the journey of *jiva* to be Shiva — the individual's absorption into the Divine. This is the goal of every individual's life.

Verse 47

īśvara uvāca
bhrānti baddho bhavet jīvah
bhrāntirmuktaḥ sadāśivāh
karyāḥ hi kāraṇaṃ tvaṃ ca
pūrna-bodha viśiṣyate

Translation

Ishwara said, "*Jiva* is bound by delusion, and when free from delusion he becomes *Sadashiva. Karya* (effect) and *karanam* (cause), is you. This is realized through complete awareness.

Metaphorical Interpretation

Ignorance of the true nature of one's Self —'Who am I?' — is the cause of suffering. Freeing oneself from this ignorance also shatters the egocentric separateness from the Divine.

Ignorance has a two-fold effect:

avarana shakti	veiling power,
vikshepa shakti	projecting power.

Ignorance covers up Truth, projecting a completely distorted idea of reality. To explain the effect of ignorance or nescience, Vedic scholars give the example of a rope in the darkness appearing as a snake. The rope appears to be a non-existent snake, creating fear in the individual's mind. In this situation, not to see the rope is the veiling power of ignorance, but to see the snake in the rope is the effect of the projecting power of ignorance. With the light of inner wisdom fear of the snake vanishes, and the rope is seen for what it really is. When ignorance, the cause, is eliminated one becomes free from individual egoistic awareness. Knowledge is the source of all cause and effect. When one is established in Self-knowledge, one realizes that all actions and causes are nothing but God. This is known as complete awareness. 'I am the body' fades and the liberated seeker realizes, 'I am Shiva, *Shivo'ham.*'

Verse 48

mano 'nyatra śivo 'nyatra
śaktiranyatra mārutah

Translation

(For a person steeped in ignorance) Mind is not here, God (Shiva) is elsewhere, so also is *shakti* as well as *marata* (breath).

Metaphorical Interpretation

Those whose mind and breath are agitated, and who perceive Shiva as separate from Shakti, are submerged in a state of ignorance. Restlessness is the cause of misery. When breath is unstable, the mind is likewise excitable and changeable and this reflects in all activities. A diversified and mutable mind cannot experience the state of Truth. A wavering and unsteady person is easily distracted; nothing is ever accomplished without concentration or singleness of purpose. In an obscure and ambiguous state, human beings always divide and differentiate, finding separateness in Shiva and Shakti. Confusion leads people to think that God is in heaven and not near to us, within us. Their ego does not let them feel the living presence of God in creation, in everybody, and in every single breath. Through breath-awareness, a sincere seeker can achieve liberation. Restlessness and oscillation is the nature of the mind, but through regular practice, self-analysis, and non-attachment, the state of unity and harmony can be experienced.

Verse 49

idaṃ tīrthaṃ idaṃ tīrtham
bhramanti tāmasā janāḥ
ātmatīrthaṃ na jānānti
kathaṃ mokṣo varānane

Translation

O Charming One (Parvati), *tamasic* (ignorant and dull witted) people go from one holy place to another in search of God, but without knowing the *atmatirtha* (seat of the soul), liberation is not possible.

Metaphorical Interpretation

Most people search for happiness and realization, but they fail to follow the path directed by the realized. Without real inner transformation, wandering in varied directions does not lead to the state of realization. Pilgrimages and dips in holy rivers are only an external play. A pilgrimage to a far off place has no significance unless the devotee is sincerely trying to change. A real pilgrimage is the inner journey that goes from the lower centers to the soul center, *atma teertha*, (place of pilgrimage, the soul). Only through this inner growth can a spiritual aspirant attain liberation. To achieve this, inner calmness, concentration, determination, and complete dedication are essential.

Verse 50

na veda vedaṃ ityāhuh
vedo brahma sanātanam
brahma vidyā rato yastu
sa vipro veda pāragāh

Translation

The Veda is not only a book, as people think, but is the eternal Brahman. One, who constantly dwells in Brahman, is the one who is really *brahmana.*

Metaphorical Interpretation

As was previously explained in earlier verses, there are four major Vedas; Rig Veda, Sama Veda, Yajur Veda, and Atharva Veda and four auxiliary Vedas: Dhanur Veda, Gandharva Veda, Sthapatya Veda, and Ayur Veda. These books contain both ephemeral and spiritual knowledge.

We also observed that the word Veda comes from the root verb *vid* i.e., 'to know.' What is to be known? Without the experiential knowledge of Brahman, all other knowledge is incomplete. A devotee who has mastered the Vedas, who is immersed in the search for Truth, is a *vipra* — a person with inner purity. Lahiri Mahasaya, a great master in the Kriya Yoga lineage, pronounced that 'Kriya is Veda.' The sincere practice of techniques like Kriya Yoga and the constant pursuit of Self-knowledge is the true spirit behind the Vedas.

Verse 51

mathitvā catura vedān
sarvaśāstrāṇi caiva hi
sāraṃ tu yogibhiḥ pītam
takraṃ pīvanti panḍitāh

Translation

Churning the four Vedas and all the scriptures, yogis drink (enjoy) the essence (butter) of the Vedas while the pundits (mere scholars) are happy with the buttermilk of book knowledge.

Metaphorical Interpretation

Cream or butter can only be obtained by churning milk or yogurt. Once butter surfaces, it cannot be mixed back into milk. Allegorically, a devotee should churn one's life to get the taste of Truth hidden within. Once Self-knowledge is attained, it is easy to swim in the ocean of the world instead of drowning. Through careful study of the four Vedas, a genuine seeker understands and accepts their essence, but a foolish one is lost in the maze of words and ideas.

The holy scriptures teach,

ananta śāstraṃ bahu veditavyam
svalpasathāyuḥ bahavaśca vighnāh

yat sāra bhūtaṃ tadupāsitavyam
hamsa yathā kṣiramivāmbu madhyāt

"The scriptures are endless, and life is short. Difficulties are many. That which is the essence, should be accepted, as the swan alone can separate the essence milk, leaving water aside."

Shastra is 'scripture.' The word consists of two parts *shah* + *astra*. *Shah* means 'cutter' and *astra* is 'weapon.' Metaphorically, it is a double-edged weapon that frees a seeker from the bondage of past and future karmas, allowing one to live in the present with strength. Another interpretation of *shastra* is — *shasanat shastra ucyate* — 'through discipline, one can wield a weapon.' Just as a king or warrior wields a weapon to eliminate evil, the seeker instilling self-discipline acquires a tool of scriptures to eradicate ignorance and lead a righteous life.

An accomplished yogi, through meditation and Self-realization, becomes established in the *so'ham* 'I am That' or *hamsa* the 'swan' state. *Paramahamsa* is the highest title given to a yogi, meaning 'supreme swan.' A scholar is referred to as *pandita*, but superficial scriptural knowledge may enhance ego, whereas true knowledge liberates the seeker. A sincere yogi knows the inner meaning and message of the scriptures, whereas an intellectual scholar is busy with the outward meaning often leading to vanity.

Verse 52

ucchiṣtaṃ sarva śāstrāṇi
sarvavidyā mukhe mukhe
no 'cchiṣtam brāhmano jñānam
avyaktaṃ cetanāmayam

Translation

The mere intellectualization of the *shastras* is of no value. The real value of Self-knowledge cannot be expressed, as it is inexpressible pure awareness.

Metaphorical Interpretation

In this verse Lord Shiva says, *ucchishtam sarva shastrani*: "All scriptures are like the left-overs on the plate and hence, considered impure." Studying and interpreting the scriptures is commonly held in high regard, but the exercise is useless unless Truth is experienced. Shiva makes clear that knowledge acquired from the scriptures must not remain only in the mouth, but should be internalized as thoughts and feelings. Truth must be realized, not just remain an intellectual activity.

Ucchista means 'left-overs in the plate after a meal.' It is considered impure and unhygienic. True knowledge of Brahman is never unclean; Self-knowledge is always undefiled.

Spiritual experience transcends mental and intellectual interpretation. In a deep state of meditation, a seeker experiences the state of reality. This is defined as pure awareness; God is felt in everything at all times.

The Bhairava Damara Tantra describes such anomaly in these words,

tamtrārtha śastravyutpātya jñātuṃ gacchati yah pumān
sa evāndho vijanīyāt uluka iva bhāskaram

"One who tries to know the meaning of the Tantras and the origin of the scriptures, is like a blind person, such as an owl searching for the sun."

The Kularnava Tantra (1:96) gives a similar interpretation,

tattvaṃ ātmasthaṃ ajñātvā mūḍha śāstreṣu yujyate
gopaḥ kukṣagataṃ chāgaṃ kupe paśyati durmatih

"Without experiencing the Truth hidden in oneself, foolish people search for it in books; like a person holding a goat in his hands, and (at the same time) looking at its image in the well."

The direct experience of Self knowledge is vital to the supreme state of realization. Instead of studying the scriptures, a seeker should put them into practice. In the Bible, it is described that the scriptures are the Breath of God, therefore with every breath, a spiritual aspirant should turn inwards and realize one's own real nature to be free.

Verse 53

na tapaḥ tapaḥ ityāhu
brahmacaryaṃ tapottamam
ūrddhvaretā bhavet yastu
sa devo natu mānuṣah

Translation

Penance is not penance as it is ordinarily thought of, and *brahmacharyam* (celibacy) is the best of all penances. One who is a perpetual celibate is not an ordinary human being, and attains godhood.

Metaphorical Interpretation

In this verse, Lord Shiva speaks of the state of *brahmacharya* to be established in God without deviation. To understand the inner meaning of this verse, three concepts need to be clear: *tapas*, *brahmacharya*, and *urdhvareta*.

Tapas means 'burning,' 'warming,' 'consumed by heat,' 'causing pain,' 'penance,' or 'religious austerity.' In spiritual practices, *tapas* is used as penance to withstand heat and cold, hunger and thirst, with endurance, while remembering God. *Tapa* is also derived from the verb *taapa,* meaning 'heat.' Body temperature is maintained through the breath. Metaphorically, to love and be constantly aware of God in every breath is also considered *tapas.*

Brahmacharya literally means 'abstinence' or 'perpetual celibacy.' Yet a married person, following certain rules and disciplines within married life, can also be considered a *brahmachari.* The inner meaning of *brahmacharya* is *brahma vicharana,* i.e., 'to roam' or 'to move in Brahman.' A *brahmachari* undertakes all activities with love for God, without any deviation. Thus, *brahmacharya* has multiple meanings: 'religious studies,' 'a life of celibacy,' or 'self-restraint' but above all it means 'constant awareness of God.'

Urdhvareta means *urdhva* or 'higher' and *reta* or 'engrossed,' or the preservation of human magnetism in the body.' In the Hindu tradition it is believed that through the practice of regular celibacy, a spiritual aspirant inwardly transforms the life-energy into *ojas*, which is translated as 'human magnetism,' or *urdhvareta*. A state of continuous cheerfulness, a peaceful countenance, and increased vitality, are signs of *ojas* in a person. It is the state of continuous awareness of the higher purpose of life, and a mind engrossed in God-consciousness. This state is synonymous with 'perfect evolution.'

Verse 54

na dhyānaṃ dhyānaṃ ityāhu
dhyānaṃ śūnyagataṃ manah
tasya dhyāna praśadena
saukhyaṃ mokṣaṃ na samśayam

Translation

***Dhyanam* is not meditation if the mind is not devoid of all thoughts. Only through such meditation, peace and liberation are obtained. There is no doubt about this.**

Metaphorical Interpretation

Dhyana or meditation is the seventh limb described in the Yoga Sutras of Patañjali. Meditation is an art of withdrawing consciousness from the mind and the senses and turning it towards the source of life, centered in the brain very close to the pineal gland. Such concentration enables the seeker to experience a state of inner peace and bliss. The highest level of such meditation ultimately results in communion with God, known as *samadhi.* According to the Yamala Tantra,

dhyānam tu dvividhā proktā sthūla sūkṣma vibhedatah

sthūlaṃ mantramayaṃ viddhi sūkṣmamśca mantravarjitam

"Meditation is said to be of two types; gross and subtle. The gross art of meditation is based on mantra while the subtle is beyond mantra.

In the scriptures it is also said,

snāna māna mala tyājya śauca indriya nigraha
abheda darśanaṃ jñānaṃ dhyānaṃ nirviṣayaṃ manah

"A true bath is to purify or cleanse the mind; true purification is the control of the senses; true knowledge is the state of unity or experiencing God everywhere; true meditation is the state beyond thoughts or objects."

Regular practice of Self-awareness focuses the mind on the goal of life. The tendencies of a restless nature disappear, and the state of inner tranquility, peace, and love is achieved. Lord Shiva teaches that the true state of meditation is to be immersed in nothingness, with the mind devoid of all thoughts.

Meditation bestows two major benefits:

i) *Saukhyam* is derived from *sukha*; *su* means 'complete,' 'good,' or 'real,' *kha* means 'space' or 'sky.' *Sukha* is therefore the 'state of happiness that can be experienced in deep meditation.' At this juncture, there is a sense of real freedom from the noose of ignorance and delusion.

ii) *Moksha* comes from *moha kshaya* — *moha* means 'delusion' and *ksha* is 'elimination.' *Moksha* signifies 'the elimination of delusion, illusion, and error.'

Verse 55

na homaṃ homaṃ ityāhu
samādhau tattu bhūyate
brahmāgnau hūyate prānam
homakarma taducyate

Translation

Homam (sacrifice) is not a *homam* in which *samadhi* (realization) is reached. *Homa karma* (sacrificial ceremony) is that process in which *prana* (breath) is offered as an oblation into *brahmagni* (the sacred fire).

Metaphorical Interpretation

Through constant practice, devotion, and deep meditation the devotee becomes saturated in spiritual experience and enters the state of spiritual ecstasy known as *samadhi. Dhi* means 'intellect,' and *sama* means 'balance.' Metaphorically, *samadhi* is not a state of intellectualization, rather it is the experience of being established in Truth; all duality disappears and only complete oneness with God remains. To go deeper in meditation and eventually attain *samadhi,* Lord Shiva teaches the art of *homa* (sacrificial fire ceremony).

In ritualistic practices, *sadhakas* perform a fire ceremony in the Vedic or Tantric tradition, offering oblations with ghee and other materials, into the blazing fire, accompanied by the chanting of mantras.

Tantric practices can be divided into two steps; the preliminary step is the practice of mantra and the ultimate step is the practice of yoga or meditation. *Homa* is both; the ritualistic offering in the external fire, and the inner offering called *pranayama,* where the oblation of *prana* or breath is offered to *brahmagni* or the sacred fire in the soul center. In this context the seven chakras are symbolically believed to be the seven ceremonial fires.

Chakra	**Name of the fire**
Sahasrara	Visvarupa maha agni
Ajna	Brahmagni
Vishuddha	Samudbhava
Anahata	Ahavaniya
Manipura	Vaishvanara
Svadhisthana	Grihapati
Muladhara	Dakshinagni

By means of an inner fire ceremony, a devotee practices *pranayama* or a special breathing technique learned directly from the guru, offering every breath as an oblation into the *brahmagni,* i.e., the *ajna chakra* (soul center) and the *sahasrara* (the crown of the head). The practice of *pranayama* enables a sincere seeker to attain the state of deep meditation and ultimately. *samadhi* or realization.

Verse 56

pāpakarma bhavet bhavyam
puṇyaṃ caiva pravartate
tasmāt sarva prayatnena
tad dravyaṃ ca tyajet budhah

Translation

By *papakarma* (sinful actions) one acquires sin, and by virtuous acts, virtue is earned. Intelligent people make every effort to discard both.

Metaphorical Interpretation

Papa (vice) and *punya* (merit) represent duality: the cause of birth and death; happiness and unhappiness; disease and health. *Papa* is literally translated as 'sin,' 'demerit,' 'vice,' or 'wrong action.' *Punya,* on the other hand is 'merit,' 'virtue,' or 'noble deed.' It has already been mentioned, in the first section of this work, how *papa* and *punya* (vice and virtue) become the cause of bondage.

Any kind of chain is difficult to break, but even though sinful activities bring suffering and should be shunned, virtuous deeds, which promote goodness, also prevent a real state of liberation.

In the Bhagavad Gita (9:21) it is said, *kṣīṇe puṇye martyalokaṃ viśanti*:

"When the fruits of the meritorious deeds are exhausted, one suffers again in the mortal plane."

A sincere seeker, whose ultimate goal is liberation, should try to be free from the clutches of both vice and virtue. *Sarva prayatnena*: 'by all efforts' — by careful and intelligent efforts it can be achieved.

Verse 57

yāvat varṇaṃ kulaṃ sarvam
tāvat jñānaṃ na jāyate
brahma jñanaṃ padamjñātvā
sarva varṇa vivarjitah

Translation

Being born in a high caste or creed does not give knowledge. Knowing the source of *brahmajñana* is beyond all caste and creed.

Metaphorical Interpretation

There is a tendency in human beings to be attracted to name and fame; caste and creed; wealth and prosperity. A truly spiritual seeker should avoid even the slightest material or worldly comfort. To illustrate this point, Lord Shiva speaks of *varna* and *kula*.

Varna — has multiple meanings: 'colour,' 'hue,' 'complexion,' 'caste,' 'class,' 'tribe,' 'letter,' 'characteristic,' or 'sound.' People may be vain about their attractive appearance. Egoistic people cherish their station if they happen to be Brahmin or born within a rich and powerful family. If people have a good education or worldly knowledge, they are fond of exhibiting this on every possible occasion. What most people do not easily recognize is that all of the above represent serious hindrances along the spiritual journey.

Kula — relates to 'race' or 'family,' a 'herd' or 'multitude,' but it also refers to the body as in 'body consciousness.' Around the world, ordinary people thrive on their dynastic fame or family fortune, but ego, vanity, and pride are the cause of all downfalls. A sincere seeker should ruthlessly shun these misguided paths, striving to remain in the state of knowledge. Lord Shiva emphasizes that in order to evolve in spirituality, *varna* and *kula* must be cast aside. A *brahmajñani* or a 'knower of Brahma,' a 'realized one' is free from all limitations, maintaining complete equanimity and perceiving the universal soul everywhere and in everything.

Verse 58

devī uvāca
yat tvayā kathitaṃ jñānam
nāhaṃ jānāmi śamkara
niścaya bruhi deveśa
mano yatra vilīyate

Translation

Devi said, "I am not able to understand this jñanam (wisdom), which you have described, O Shankara. Please tell me clearly, Lord of lords, how does the mind get dissolved?"

Metaphorical Interpretation

This verse addresses the quest of a seeker in the search of knowledge, but Parvati is not asking for theoretical knowledge, she seeks practical experience. At the stage where the play of the mind is no longer required, the mind is dissolved.

Each sense has a presiding deity, but all the senses derive their strength and energy from the light of the soul. The One Soul (Shiva) is *devesha,* or the Lord of all gods.

Verse 59

īśvara uvāca
mano vākyaṃ tathā karma
tṛtīyaṃ yatra vilīyate
vinā svapnaṃ yathā nidrā
brahmajñānaṃ taducyate

Translation

Ishwara said, "A state in which mind, speech, and action are dissolved, and where one experiences the awareness of dreamless deep sleep, is the state of *brahmajñanam*."

Metaphorical Interpretation

Science speaks of the evolution of life on the planet earth, while spirituality explains the evolution of consciousness in each living being. In this verse, Lord Shiva refers to the highest state of evolution, which is a result of conscious and continuous effort.

The concept of *tri — karana* or the 'three instruments' encompasses thought, speech, and action. The purpose of the mind is to think; of speech is to communicate; and of action is to accomplish various goals in the material as well as the spiritual world. The three concepts, therefore, represent thoughts, words, and deeds.

First comes the sublimation of the mind and then its dissolution. Through the practice of spirituality, impurity in the mind is eliminated, allowing the mind to regain its original peacefulness. In order to acquire control over speech, it is important to speak truthfully, lovingly, and for the good of others. It is also helpful to observe silence regularly; this is a training ground for the mind and tongue. All activities performed through the senses, should be an act of yoga directed towards the union, avoiding trouble or disunity.

The Viveka Chudamani teaches, *cittasya shuddhaye karma:* "All activities should aim at inner purification." It is essential to follow the spiritual teachings of the guru regularly and sincerely with love and devotion. Only in this way can a devotee attain the state where all the instruments (mind, speech, and action) become redundant, or non-existent.

Lord Shiva compares deep meditation to a dreamless sleep

as an external allegory to explain the state of the dawn of knowledge. If meditation is accompanied by thoughts, it becomes similar to a sleep full of dreams. Knowledge of Brahman can only be achieved when the sincere meditator, filled with inner purity, goes beyond the mind.

Verse 60

ekākī nispṛhaḥ śāntah
cintā-nidrā-vivarjitāh
bālabhāvaḥ tathā bhāvo
brahmajñānaṃ taducyate

Translation

Remaining secluded; free from desires; peaceful; devoid of thoughts and sleep; with the attitude of a child; is the state of *brahmajñanam.*

Metaphorical Interpretation

This verse offers a concise explanation of the state of Self-realization. In order to obtain spiritual evolution, Lord Shiva elucidates on the following requirements:

i) *Ekaki* means 'alone' or 'secluded.' Most human beings seek the company of each other. Living alone is a painful burden. Loneliness brings on sadness and even depression. But a spiritual seeker likes to be alone. To live in seclusion is to develop the art of Self-mastery. Seclusion becomes the price of greatness. Internally, to be free from thoughts is the true meaning of seclusion. If the mind is truly free, nothing can disrupt it.

ii) *Nispriha* means 'lack of desires or ambition.' Expectation is the propelling force behind the cycle of birth and death. The only way to break this vicious cycle is to ruthlessly analyze the needs we have in life and eliminate all unnecessary desires. The world is full of transitory worldly pleasures, unless a devotee firmly upholds *nispriha*; the state of *brahmajñanam* will always be elusive.

iii) *Shanta* is equivalent to 'peacefulness.' The Sanskrit word is derived from the root word *shama* i.e., 'control of the mind and senses.' Ordinarily, the mind is turbulent and the senses are restless. But rigorous discipline helps to promote the state of peace.

iv) *Chinta vivarjita* literally means 'free from worries and emotions.' Through the practice of breath regulation, inner tranquility can be procured. Breath-control leads to mind-control.

v) *Nidra vivarjita* means 'free from lethargy,' 'laziness' and even 'sleep.' Sleep is a state of pervasive ignorance.

vi) *Bala bhava* is known as a 'childlike state.' Spiritually evolved people have a childlike attitude, devoid of worry, expectation, or negative qualities. Jesus often said that a child could enter the Kingdom of Heaven.

All these indicators are permanently seen in spiritually advanced people who live immersed in a life of completeness and love.

Verse 61

ślokārdhena pravakṣāmi
yaduktaṃ tattva-darśibhih
sarva cintā parityāgo
niścinto yoga ucyate

Translation

I will explain in a nutshell all that has been said by seers and sages. Yoga is that state where giving up all thought, one is established in a thoughtless state.

Metaphorical Interpretation

Tattvadarshi is a person who has experienced the state of Truth, becoming established in wisdom. Through the practice of yoga and meditatio n it is possible to secure fulfillment.

In this verse, Lord Shiva gives a precise explanation of the path of yoga. Yoga is not only a path; it is also a way of life. Since yoga is the state of complete tranquility, devoid of all thought, it automatically leads to the ultimate state of experience.

Sage Patañjali described yoga in the following terms, *yogaḥ citta vritti nirodhah*: "The art of eliminating thought waves."

The Bhagavad Gita has numerous definitions of yoga,

yogaḥ karmasu kauśalam:	"Perfection in action is yoga" (2:50).
samatvaṃ yoga ucyate:	"Equanimity is yoga" (2:48).
viyogaṃ yoga sangitam:	"Separation from duality is yoga" (6:23).

In the Shvetashvatara Upanishad (2:4), yoga is described as, *yuktena manasa:* "Yoga is the state of uniting the mind with the Supreme."

The world and worldly activities are below the *ajna chakra,* in the five lower centers. When the mind is filled with mundane matters it becomes restless, turbulent, and ambitious, leading to endless activities and conflicting emotions. But if the mind rises towards the *ajna chakra*, becoming peaceful and tranquil, it is freed from negative propensities. Once attention is fixed in the *sahasrara,* the mind dissolves into nothingness.

Lord Shiva defines yoga as the art of the evolution of consciousness — from restlessness to calmness, and ultimately to the state of *samadhi,* or complete union with God. Yoga is the state of freedom from the restless play of the mind.

Verse 62

nimiṣaṃ nimiṣārdhaṃ vā
samādhiṃ adhigacchati
śatajanmārjitaṃ pāpam
tatkṣaṇāt devi naśyati

Translation

O Devi, if *samadhi* (realization) is attained even for a second or a split second, the sins accrued over a hundred births, can be destroyed instantly.

Metaphorical Interpretation

The experience of *samadhi* can last for a single moment or for a prolonged period of time, bringing with it the transcendental state of superconsciousness and perfect union with the Absolute. Such an experience transforms a person completely. There is no longer any separateness, only oneness with God and the entire creation, which ultimately brings love and eternal bliss.

To grasp this point more clearly, two concepts, *samadhi* and *papa* need more elaboration:

1) *Samadhi* is made up of *sam* +*a* +*dha* + *kvip*. *Sam* means 'completely' or 'beautifully,' *a* is 'to bring' or 'to uplift,' *dha* is 'to behold' or 'to establish,' and *kvip* is 'the state.' Therefore *samadhi* means 'a state where there is complete establishment of consciousness in the indwelling Self.'

The word has many additional meanings such as 'collecting,' 'composing,' 'concentrating,' 'profound or abstract meditation,' 'concentration of the mind on one object,' 'perfect absorption of thought in one object of meditation, known as the Supreme.'

Samadhi also means continuous balance of *dhi*, or 'the intellect,' a state of perfect equanimity. It is the last limb of yoga described by Patañjali. *Samadhi* can only be experienced as the result of sincere practice and deep meditation.

2) *Papam — pāti rakṣati asmat atmānaṁ* — means 'the cause of downfall and destruction.' The literal translation is 'evil,' 'sinful,' 'wicked,' 'vicious,' 'mischievous,' 'destructive,' 'inauspicious,' 'malignant,' or 'bad fortune.'

Individuals are made up of karma accumulated from past lives; karma produces *punya* or 'merit' and *papa* or 'demerit.' Positive activities breed good results and sinful actions produce suffering. Positive and negative karma does not balance or neutralize each other. The role of karma has to be played out.

However, in this verse, Lord Shiva assures his devotees that to become established in *samadhi,* even for a brief second in time can give lasting freedom from the accumulated sins over a hundred lifetimes. Purity and eternal love are the very essence of spiritual life. Encouraging a seeker to go beyond vice and virtue eventually will lead to liberation.

Verse 63

devī uvāca
kasya nāma bhavet śaktih
kasya nāma bhavet śivah
etanme bruhi me deva
paścāt jñānaṃ prakāśaya

Translation

Devi asked, "Whose name is Shakti, who is known as Shiva, O Lord? Please tell me through what (path) is knowledge illuminated."

Metaphorical Interpretation

In this verse, the Divine Mother asks three questions:

i) What is Shakti?
ii) Who is Shiva?
iii) What is the path of knowledge?

Shakti is derived from the root verb *śak*, meaning 'to be able' or 'capable of.' Thus *shakti* is the state of 'ability' or 'capability.' In each living being the life-energy is manifested within the five elements, in different ways. Like the nature of fire or the properties of water, *shakti* is the strength that brings activity into life. Shiva is the beholder of *shakti* (energy or strength). Shiva is the Soul. In the absence of Shiva (Soul) the body is dead or *shava.* The path of knowledge allows the spiritual seeker to ultimately attain liberation.

God is the source of infinite knowledge. Knowledge itself is divided into *paravidya* or 'supreme knowledge' and *aparavidya* or 'material science.' The Mundaka Upanishad teaches that a sincere aspirant should strive to acquire both branches of knowledge, yet a desire to learn *paravidya* indicates spiritual progress. *Paravidya* or supreme knowledge should ideally be combined with *aparavidya* or material science.

Verse 64

īśvara uvāca
calat citte vaset śaktih
sthira citte vaset śivāh
sthira citto bhavet devi
sa dehastho 'pi siddhyati

Translation

Ishwara said, "O Devi, *shakti* resides in the restless, active mind and Shiva resides in the tranquil mind. The state of steady memory is itself Devi (or Parvati). One who is established in the tranquil mind becomes realized while living in the body."

Metaphorical Interpretation

Any external notion is possible due to the activity of breathing, an active breath allows human beings to accomplish numerous material endeavours. This is the play of energy or *shakti;* the active mind is the seat of *shakti,* which in turn is manifested through the breath. When the breath is agitated, the mind is also restless and this is reflected in a chaotic lifestyle. But when the breath is tranquil, the mind becomes pacified and the seeker is able to experience divinity. *Sthira citto bhavet devi*: "The state of steady memory is itself Devi (or Parvati)." The meaning of Devi here is 'divine illumination.'

Once the breath is regulated, the spiritual seeker becomes more peaceful, and is able to experience Truth — I am Shiva — *shivo'ham.* This is the reason why Ishwara says, "Shiva resides in the tranquil breath and the tranquil mind. Through inner tranquility a sincere devotee realizes the Self."

Through constant and continuous remembrance of the inner Self, which essentially is nothing but Devi (or Parvati), a seeker experiences divine illumination. By the practice of breath-control and God consciousness in every breath, the spiritual aspirant is able to attain the state of realization, while remaining in the body. So the art of self-evolution depends upon the regulation of breath and the sublimation of the mind.

Verse 65

devī uvāca
kasmin sthāne tridhā śaktih
ṣaṭ cakraṃ ca tathaiva ca
eko vimśati brahmāṇdam
sapta pātāla meva ca

Translation

Devi said, "In which places are the three *shaktis*, where are the six chakras situated, what are the twenty-one *brahmandas* (macrocosms) and the seven *patalas* (under worlds)?"

Metaphorical Interpretation

The questions formulated by the Divine Mother bring further light into the hidden spiritual Truth. Previously, Parvati enquired about *shakti*, Shiva and the path of knowledge. In this verse, she would like to know more about *shakti* (energy), the chakras (energy centers), and *brahmanda* (the cosmos).

The questions addressed to Lord Shiva are:

i) Where is the seat of the three *shaktis*?

ii) What are the six *chakras*?

iii) What are the *brahmandas*?

iv) Which are the *patalas* (lower planes) in the body?

Verse 66

īśvara uvāca
urdhva śaktir bhavet kantha
adhaḥ śaktir bhavet guhyah
madhya śaktir bhavet nābhih
śaktyātītaṃ nirañjanam

Translation

Ishwara said, "*Urdhva shakti* (the energy for upward propensities) is in the *kantha* (neck center), *adhah shakti*

(the energy for lower activities) is in the coccyx center, and *madhya shakti* (the energy for moderate activities), is at the *nabhi* (navel center). One who is beyond these *shaktis,* is the Formless."

Metaphorical Interpretation

As described earlier, *shakti* is the energy or consciousness permeating all levels of life. The energy or life-force is symbolized by the feminine attributes of the Hindu trinity; Brahma the creator, Vishnu the sustainer, and Shiva the destroyer. In the body, *shakti* or energy is divided into three:

i) *Urddhva shakti*	Energy for evolution,
ii) *Madhya shakti*	Energy for maintenance,
iii) *Adhah shakti*	Energy for lower activities.

Urddhva shakti remains in the upper part of the body, promoting spiritual evolution. When consciousness is brought to the higher planes of existence, a step forward is made towards the state of spiritual evolution. This energy is also known as Mahakali, another name for Parvati, the divine consort of Lord Shiva.

Madhya shakti is the energy that sustains the life-force within the body through *prana,* and is manifested by the breath, the intake of food, and the process of digestion and assimilation. This energy remains in the middle part of the body, and is otherwise known as Mahalakshmi, the divine consort of Lord Vishnu.

Adhah shakti is the lower aspect of energy, which sustains the creative and productive aspects of life, through material and sexual experience. This form of energy is concentrated in the lower centers and is known as Mahasaraswati, the divine consort of Brahma, who assists him in the process of creation.

Although *shakti* works in three different ways, it is essentially one and non-dual; it is the power of Brahman, the Absolute. Brahman is beyond everything, being Supreme and Formless.

Tri Shakti	Place of Manifestation	Trinity	Name of Divine Consort
Urddhva shakti	*Vishuddha/Ajna*	Shiva	Mahakali
Madhya shakti	*Manipura/Anahata*	Vishnu	Mahalakshmi
Adhah shakti	*Muladhara/Svadhisthana*	Brahma	Mahasaraswati

Verse 67

ādhāra guhyacakramtu
svādhishtānaṃ ca liṅgakam
cakrabhedaṃ mayākhyātam
cakratītaṃ namonamah

Translation

The *muladhara* is the bottom center. The genital center is *svadhisthana.* I have explained the different chakras to you. Pray to the One, who is beyond the chakras.

Metaphorical Interpretation

In this verse, Lord Shiva replies to the question regarding the six chakras:

Guhya (anus)	*Muladhara*
Linga (genital)	*Svadhisthana*
Nabhi (navel)	*Manipura*
Hridaya (heart)	*Anahata*
Kantha (neck)	*Vishuddha*
Bhrumadhya (soul)	*Ajna*

The six chakras are the dwelling place of energy and its manifestation, action, and enjoyment. But beyond the chakras is the Un-manifested, the Absolute, which can be realized through *shat-chakrabheda* — or penetrating into the veil of energy and going to the state of *chakratita,* i.e., beyond everything. This is the state of union between Shiva and Shakti, the state of absolute awareness.

Verse 68

kāyordhvaṃ ca brahmalokah
svādhāḥ patālameva ca
ūrddhva mūlaṃ adhaḥ śākham
vṛkṣākāraṃ kaḷebaram

Translation

The upper part of the body is *brahmaloka* and the bottom portion is *patala.* The body is like (an inverted) tree with roots at the top and branches hanging down.

Metaphorical Interpretation

The outer universe and the universe within have similar characteristics. The entire cosmos is represented within the human body. Each body is divided into three parts:

i)	*Kayordha*	the upper part of the body *brahmaloka,*
ii)	*Kaya madhya*	the middle part of the body *bhuloka,*
iii)	*Kaya adhah*	the lower part of the body *patala.*

The upper part of the body is measured from the midpoint of the eyebrows *(bhrumadhya)* to the fontanel (*brahma randhra*). This is the location of the *sahasrara chakra.* A sincere seeker should keep one's concentration fixed on the fontanel, i.e., *brahmaloka,* the abode of Brahman.

In the last part of the verse, Lord Shiva compares the body with an inverted tree. Although the Bhagavad Gita (15:1) and the Katha Upanishad (2:3:1) speak of a tree, they never openly compare the body with an inverted tree.

Tree, in Sanskrit, is *vriksha,* which is derived from the root verb *vrks* — meaning 'to receive' or 'to cover.' Therefore the body is just a cover for the soul. Each human body is an inverted tree, the roots remaining at the top and the trunk and the branches flowing downwards. The root of life and activities, as well as the root of knowledge and liberation, is stored in the upper part of the body, which is *brahmaloka.* The root and the source are one and the same.

Verse 69

devī uvāca
śiva śamkara īśāna
brūhi me parameśvara
daśa vāyuḥ kathaṃ deva
daśadvārāṇi caiva hi

Translation

Devi said, "O Shiva, Shankara, Ishana (who remains in the vacuum), Parameshwara, Deva, please tell me what are the ten *vayus* (winds) and the ten doors of the body."

Metaphorical Interpretation

In this verse Parvati uses four different names to address Lord Shiva:

i) Shiva — *shyati papam* — One who eliminates vices and is

always auspicious, bestowing goodness.

Metaphorically — *shava* (dead body) + i (*shakti*) is none other than the union of body and soul or Shiva.

ii) Shankara — *sham-sukham karoti* — One who confers happiness or prosperity.

iii) Ishana — from the root verb *ish* — 'to rule' or 'to master' — One who is the 'Lord and the Master of life.'

iv) Parameshwara — *parama* (supreme) + *ishwara* (Lord) — One who is omnipotent and extremely powerful.

v) Deva — *div* means 'illuminating' as well as 'formless as the sky.' Deva here represents — One who is formless as well as 'divine intelligence.'

Parvati's question about the ten *vayus* (literally meaning winds but metaphorically symbolizing vital breaths), and the ten doors in the body is answered in the following verse.

Verse 70

īśvara uvāca
hṛdi prānaḥ sthito vāyuh
apāno guhya samsthītāh
samāno nābhideśetu
udānaḥ kaṇṭham āśritah

Translation

Ishwara said, "There are ten vayus; the *vayu* (wind) in the heart is *prana, apana* is present in the bottom, *samana* is in the navel, and *udana* stays around the neck."

Metaphorical Interpretation

In this verse Lord Shiva points out the location of four vayus or vital breaths within the body.

i) *Prana:* has many meanings such as 'breath,' 'life,' 'the vital breath that keeps the heart and lungs functioning,' 'energy,' 'the soul.' *Prana,* interpreted as the life-force, resides in the heart (*anahata* or heart center). It helps in maintaining life, as well as in the digestive process, and keeps the body active.

ii) *Apana: a* means 'not' and *pana* means 'to drink.' So *apana* means 'that which is not taken in or inhaled.' This *vayu* (breath) remains in the *muladhara* or bottom center, and it is instrumental in excretion.

iii) *Samana:* literally means 'making equal' or 'balanced.' This *vayu* has its seat in the *manipura* or navel center and is essential for digestion.

iv) *Udana:* literally means 'breathing upward'— *ut* 'upward,' and *ana* 'to bring.' *Udana* is therefore the vital breath that rises from the throat and enters the head. This *vayu* is seated in the *vishuddha* or neck center. There is a detailed description of this *prana* in the Taittiriya Upanishad.

Verse 71

vyānaḥ sarva gato dehe
sarva gātreṣu samsthitah
nāgaḥ ūrdhva gato vāyuh
kūrma tīrthāṇi samsthitāh

Translation

Vyana is present in all bodies, in the neck region, naga moves upwards and kurma is present in the tirthas (sex organs).

Metaphorical Interpretation

Lord Shiva describes the seat of three more *pranas* or vital breaths in the body:

v) *Vyana*: has no particular area in which it is confined but remains rather diffused in the entire body.

vi) *Naga:* is one of the vital breaths expelled when there is an erection; it is an upward moving *prana.*

vii) *Kurma:* is the vital energy or breath in the abdominal region, which influences the menstrual cycle in women and the ejaculation of semen in men. It is present in the *thirtas* or sex organs.

Verse 72

krukaraḥ kṣobhite caiva
devadatto'pi jṛmbhaṇe
dhanañjayo nādaghoṣe
niviśeccaiva śāmyati

Translation

***Krukarah* functions while there is shivering and trembling in the body, *devadatta* is present in (the act of) yawning, and *dhananjaya* is responsible for (making) sound.**

Metaphorical Interpretation

The last three of the ten prominent *vayus* (vital airs) are:

viii) *Krukara* — is the vital breath in the chest, which regulates emotion, and specifically shivering and trembling.

ix) *Devadatta* — is the vital energy situated in the lungs, which facilitates the act of yawning.

x) *Dhananjaya* — located at the throat, this vital air is responsible for sound, speech, and conversation.

Verse 73

evaṃ vāyur nirālambo
yogīnāṃ yoga sammataḥ
navadvāraṃ ca pratyakṣam
daśamaṃ manaḥ ucyate

Translation

Those who ascend the path of yoga become independent of these *vayus* (vital airs). The nine doors of the body are directly perceived, while the tenth door is the mind.

Metaphorical Interpretation

The breath or in a subtle way *prana,* regulates the human mind and its activities. Yogis who sincerely practice the art of breath-control, regulate their life and ultimately ascend in the path of yoga. Even a yogi of the highest order uses complete control over *prana,* during deep meditation and *samadhi.*

In order to attain such a summit, a yogi has to lead a life of self-discipline and complete self-control, while possessing a proper understanding of life (knowledge combined with wisdom). Self-discipline is a mixture of harmony and moderation. This inner awareness is translated in every thought, word, and activity.

In yogic language, the act of disciplining the mind and the senses is known as *dvara* or 'the doors of perception and expression.' Lord Shiva explains that each human body is a 'temple with ten doors,' i.e., two eyes; two nostrils; two ears; the mouth; the genital organs; and the anus. The tenth door is *brahma randhra* (the fontanel), but in this text Lord Shiva speaks of the mind as the tenth door.

Nine of these doors are related to the sense organs, the external instruments of perception and expression. The mind is the internal instrument or the inner door of all experiences. When the mind is peaceful and focused, the spiritual seeker achieves the state of cosmic consciousness. The mind holds the key that enables a devotee to reach the state of highest experience.

Verse 74

devī uvāca
nāḍi bhedaṃ ca brūhi me
sarva gātreṣu samsthitam
śakti kuṇḍalinī caiva
prasūtā daśa nāḍikāh

Translation

Devi said, "Tell me about the different *nadis* (energy channels) present in the body and about the *kundalini shakti,* which manifests through the ten major *nadis* (nerve channels)."

Metaphorical Interpretation

Once the question of the ten *vayus* and the ten doors is settled, Parvati enquires about:

i) *Nadibedha:* the different *nadis* or pranic channels in the body;

ii) *Kundalini shakti:* the coiled power of the central nervous system that permeates through the ten *nadis.*

Nadi, in Sanskrit, means 'tubular organs of the body,' including 'veins,' 'arteries,' 'nerves,' and even 'subtle yogic or pranic channels.' The location of these passages is known by their pulsation or vibratory force. There is difference in opinion among yogis regarding the number of *nadis* in the body. Ordinarily, life energy flows down through these *nadis,* helping to accomplish different activities in the body. In each human being, a reservoir of spiritual energy lies untapped and hidden in a dormant state, which is described as *kuṇdalini shakti* (literally coiled energy).

Verse 75

īśvara uvāca
īḍā ca piñgalā caiva
suṣumnā ūrdhva gāminī
gāndharī hasti-jihvā ca
prasārāgamanāyatā

Translation

Ishwara said, "*Ida, pingala,* and *sushumna* move upwards while *gandhari, hasti-jihva,* and *prasara* move downwards."

Metaphorical Interpretation

The three major *nadis* are the *ida,* the *pingala,* and the *sushumna*, which are described as the channels of evolution or *urdhvaga.* These three channels are actively engaged in the process of breathing, while other *nadis* are carriers of pranic energy. Through the proper art of breathing, as taught by a qualified teacher, a devotee can achieve spiritual evolution.

Ida	located in the left side of the spine ending in the left nostril	*Chandra nadi* (lunar channel)
Pingala	located in the right side of the spine ending in the right nostril	*Surya nadi* (solar channel)
Sushumna	located in the center of the spine with equal breath in both nostrils	*Agni nadi* (fire channel)
Gandhari	located in the left eye	Contraction
Hastijihva	from the neck to the left foot	Expansion
Prasara	covering the body	Useful in movement

Verse 76

aḷambuṣā yaśā caiva
dakṣiṇāṅge ca samsthitā
kuhūśca śamkhinī caiva
vāmāṅge ca vyavasthitā

Translation

***Alambusa* and *yasha* are present in the right side of the body; *kuhu* and *shankhini* are in the left side of the body.**

Metaphorical Interpretation

alambusa	present in the right part of the body, for facial beauty,
yasha or *yasasvini*	present in the right part of the body, for prosperity,
kuhu	present in the left abdomen and ending in the genitals, for sexual pleasure,
shankhini	present in the left abdomen and ending in the anus, for excretion.

Verse 77

etāṣu daśanāḍīṣu
nānā nāḍi prasūtikā
dvi saptati sahasrāṇi
śarire nāḍikāḥ smṛtā

Translation

These ten *nadis* give birth to many different *nadis* and there are a total of about 72,000 *nadis* in the body.

Metaphorical Interpretation

The human body consists of a network of nerves or pranic channels. These nerves originate in the brain, or the seat of the soul and are distributed to the remaining parts of the body, helping to regulate all the different links and their corresponding functions. *Nadis* are instrumental in our perception of the world and play an important role in spiritual evolution. Both Tantra and Yoga emphasize the need to awaken the latent energy, which lies dormant within the *nadis* (and their respective chakras), in order to grow spiritually and attain a state of altered consciousness or enlightenment.

In the Upanishads, there is often a difference of opinion regarding the quantity of *nadis*. The following examples illustrate this:

The Chandogya Upanishad (8:6:6) describes,

śataṃ caikā ca hṛdayasya nāḍyah
tāsāṃ mūrdhānāṃ abhiniḥṣṛtaikā
tayordhvaṃ āyann amṛtatvaṃ eti
viṣuaṅṅ anyā utkrāmaṇe bhavanti
utkrāmaṇe bhavanti

"There are 101 *nadis* of the heart; one of them leads up to the crown of the head. Going upwards through that, one becomes immortal; the others flow in various other directions."

The Prashna Upanishad (3:6) gives a mathematical estimate: "There are 101 principal *nadis*. To each one of them belong 100 smaller *nadis*. To each of these belong 72,000 *nadis*. Within the *nadis* moves the diffused breath."

101 — principal *nadis*

101 x 100 = 10,100 smaller *nadis*

101 x 100 x 72,000 = 727,200,000 subtler *nadis*

In the body, the total number of nadis are 727,210,201.

The Shiva Samhita (2:13) on the other hand points out,

sārdha lakṣa trayaṃ nāḍyāṃ santi dehāntare nṛṇām
pradhānā bhutā nāḍyāstu tāsu mukhyā caturdaśa

"In the body of the human being there are 3,500,000 *nadis*, out of which fourteen are important."

It should be understood that *nadis* are interwoven like threads in a piece of cloth; pervading the whole body. In this verse, Lord Shiva alludes to 72,000 *nadis* within the body. The fourteen most prominent *nadis* described in the Shiva Samhita are:

ida, pingala, sushumna, gandhari, hastijihva, kuhu, sarasvati, pusha, shankhini, payasvini, varuni, alambusa, visvadari, and *yasasvini.*

But in the previous verses, Lord Shiva emphasized only ten principal nadis:

Ida — starts in the lower part of the spine, at the *muladhara chakra* and ends in the left nostril. This canal can create a feeling of confusion and laziness, but also has the ability of regulating the mind. The literal meaning is 'refreshment and praise.' Another name is *chandra nadi* or lunar channel.

Pingalà is situated in the right part of the spine, at the *muladhara chakra* and comes up to the right nostril. This canal can create a feeling of excessive activity. The literal meaning is 'reddish brown.' It is also known as *surya nadi* or solar channel.

Sushumna is the channel of fire that runs from the *muladhara chakra* to *sahasrara chakra* or crown of the head. The *Sushumna nadi* is by far the most important, it is also known as *moksha marga* or 'the path of liberation,' leading to Brahman or the Absolute. The literal meaning is 'a ray of the sun' (Bhagavatam 2:2:24).

Gandhari leads up from the eyes to the ears, literally meaning 'the music and dance of the celestials.' It is described in both the Goraksha Shatakam and the Darshana Upanishad.

Hastijihva runs down from the neck to the big toes. The literal meaning is 'an elephant's tongue.'

Kuhu runs from the back of the *sushumna* canal and extends to the genital(s) for ejaculation and then to the anus for excretion. The literal meaning is 'the start of the new moon.'

Shankhini runs from the left ear to the lower centers. The literal meaning is 'female spirit.'

Alambusa regulates the lower abdomen, eyes, ears, and mouth. It literally means 'a line of water.'

Yashasvini is located between the *pusha* and the *pingala nadis,* extending upwards to the ears and causing delight in praise.

Prasara pervades in the entire body and stimulates movement and the sense of touch.

Verse 78

eta yo viṇdate devi
sa yogī yoga lakṣaṇah
jñāna nāḍi bhavet devi
yogināṃ siddhidāyinī

Translation

O Devi, the one who possesses this knowledge is a yogi with all the qualities of Yoga. The *jñana nadi* (the nerve channel of knowledge) bestows perfection to the yogi.

Metaphorical Interpretation

The *jñana nadi* is more commonly known as the *sushumna,* the most important astral passage. It is the central channel through which energy or *shakti* flows to produce *samadhi* or cosmic consciousness. The *sushumna* goes straight up the interior of the spine and is referred to as the path of Brahman. The key to this verse lies with the word *vindate,* which means 'finding and gaining.' The spiritual seeker who finds the location of the *nadis,* gaining subsequent mastery over one's activities, becomes a fulfilled yogi.

A real yogi or tantric knows the play of the *nadis* and the art of mastering their functions. Through the practice of yogic exercises and breath-regulation, under the direct supervision of the guru, a yogi or tantric acquires self-control and proceeds to find union with Brahman, or the Absolute.

Unfortunately the *ida* and the *pingala* create laziness (confusion) and restlessness (over-activity), and therefore have a tendency to close the path of *sushumna.* But a sincere yogi, through regular practice, will open up the *sushumna* and roam upwards to the abode of Brahman. In the *sushumna* is a finer corridor called *vajrini nadi*, and inside this is an even more subtle passageway called *chitrini nadi*.

Vajra means 'strong determination' or 'will-power' and *chitra* means 'the shining canal.' Through navigation of these energy channels, a yogi gains perfection.

Verse 79

devī uvāca
bhutānātha mahādeva
bṛhi me parameśvara
trayadevāḥ kathaṃ deva
trayo bhavāḥ trayoguṇāh

Translation

Devi asked, "O Bhutanatha, Mahadeva, Parameshwara, please tell me who are the three *devas* (gods), the three *bhavas* (attitudes), and the three *gunas* (qualities)."

Metaphorical Interpretation

In this verse, Parvati addresses her husband as:

i) Bhutanatha — Lord of the five *bhutas* or 'elements,' such as earth, water, fire, air, and space. These elements are found in the universe, as well as in the body of all living beings. Metaphorically, Bhutanatha is 'One who brings freedom by eliminating the impact of past karma.'

ii) Mahadeva — is the great Lord or Lord of liberation.

iii) Parameshwara — is Supreme Lord.

She asks about:

i) *traya deva*	Three devas,
ii) *traya bhava*	Three attitudes,
iii) *traya guna*	Three qualities.

Verse 80

īśvara uvāca
rajobhāva sthito brahmā
sattvabhāva sthito harih
krodhabhāva sthito rudrah
trayodevāḥ trayo guṇāh

Translation

Ishwara said, "*In rajobhava* (activity, restlessness) is present Brahma (the creator), in *sattvabhava* (calmness) is Hari (Vishnu the preserver), in *krodhabhava* (anger) is present Rudra (Shiva the destroyer). These are the three *devas* and three *gunas.*

Metaphorical Interpretation

Bhava is a complex word in Sanskrit, with multiple meanings such as 'status,' 'reality,' 'condition,' 'sincerity,' 'devotion,' 'temperament,' 'disposition,' 'feeling,' 'inclination of the mind,' and so on. In this verse *bhava* indicates 'nature' or 'quality.' The Hindu Trinity, Brahma, Vishnu, and Shiva are the Lords of the three aspects of life: creation, sustenance, and destruction. Life, itself, is manifested in a cycle — with creation comes the need for maintenance, and after a certain lapse of time, creation comes to its end and is destroyed in order to be created again and again, in a purer form.

Brahma (Prajapati)	Creator	Rajas	Activity
Vishnu (Narayana)	Sustainer	Sattva	Calmness
Shiva (Rudra)	Destroyer	Tamas	Restfulness

Brahma as creator is a symbol of activity. Activity or

restlessness is *rajasic* in nature — *rajo ragatmakam viddi* — *rajas* produces likes and dislikes, leading to attachment.

Vishnu is in charge of the preservation of creation. In order to manage this task, calmness is needed to maintain peace, and accumulate strength and vitality.

Rudra (or Shiva) is the destroyer. Some anger is needed to dissolve creation. But in the end dissolution can also mean liberation as the cycle continues, until perfection is achieved. In the yogic scriptures it is said, *ye rudrah te khalu pranah:* "Rudra is none but *prana.*" In this way Rudra is the cause of death but also the means to liberation. In yogic terms, breath-control opens the door to Self-realization.

Krodha — can be understood as *ka* + *rodha, ka* means 'creation' and *rodh* means 'to block,' 'stop,' or 'obstruct.' Once activity ceases, there is a state of rest. Through the help of *prana,* a spiritual seeker can cease all activity and attain a state of complete rest and calmness, in direct union with the Absolute.

Verse 81

eka mūrtiḥ trayodevāh
brahmā-viṣṇu-maheśvarah
nānā bhāvaṃ mano yasya
tasya muktirnajāyate

Translation

All the three devas: Brahma, Vishnu, and Maheshwara (Shiva) are (in reality) one. Those who perceive a difference between them, will not achieve liberation.

Metaphorical Interpretation

Although Brahma, Vishnu, and Shiva (Maheshwara) appear to be different due to the diversity in their nature, essentially they are one and the same. Just as *om* is composed of three letters, *a, u, m,* the eternal sound. Ignorance, or dogmatic ideas, brings about differences. Multiplicity or diversity implies richness of creation. But the sense of duality also becomes the cause of bondage, fear, and delusion. To resurrect one from this fear is the experience of unity and oneness, otherwise known as *advaita.* It is the state of freedom, peace, and liberation.

Creation, maintenance, and dissolution are the play of the Absolute or Brahman. Each phase merges in the other, to form a single entity. A sincere seeker must learn to see divinity, in all these different states, to achieve liberation.

Verse 82

vīrya rūpī bhavet brahmā
vāyu rūpa sthito harih
mano rūpa sthito rudrah
trayo devaḥ trayo guṇāh

Translation

Brahma is in the form of creative force (*Virya*). *Vayu* (vital breath) is in the form of Hari. Rudra is in the form of the mind. The three *devas* are the three *gunas.*

Metaphorical Interpretation

In this verse, the particular nature of the Hindu Trinity and their symbolical location, within the body, is portrayed. *Virya* is the symbol of creation, literally meaning 'seed' or 'semen.'

Brahma, therefore, remains in the second lowest chakra in the spine (*svadhisthana*), as the presiding deity of reproduction. *Virya* alludes to 'strength,' 'heroic nature,' 'vitality,' and 'creativity.' Brahma, being the Lord of creation, is described as *virya*.

Vayu means 'that which blows.' Air is constantly in motion; the wind blows outside just as the breath flows in and out of the body. Breath sustains the life-principle, becoming the most vital aspect concerning the preservation of life's energy within the body. Since the lungs and heart regulate the breath, the air element resides in the heart center or *anahata chakra*. This chakra is the seat of Vishnu, Lord of sustenance and maintenance.

The third aspect, Rudra, the Lord of dissolution or liberation, is described as *mano rupa* — 'the form of the mind.' *Mano* is derived from *mana* 'the mind'. The mind plays a double role: a calm mind is the cause of liberation but a restless mind produces suffering. The brain is the location of the play of the mind, which is limitless. Thus Rudra (Shiva) remains in the region between the *vishuddha* (throat center) and the *ajna chakra* (the soul center), located mid-point between the eyebrows.

The three deities are related to the three *gunas*, or modes of nature. Each individual has these three qualities (*sattva, rajas,* and *tamas*). In the next verse Lord Shiva elaborates on the three *gunas* and their connection to the three deities in the Hindu Trinity.

Verse 83

dayā bhāva sthito brahmā
śuddha bhāva sthito harih
agni bhāva sthito rudrah
trayo devaḥ trayo guṇāh

Translation

Brahma is present in the quality of compassion. Hari is present in purity, and Rudra is present in the brilliance of fire. The three *devas* are the three *gunas*.

Metaphorical Interpretation

The three qualities of the Hindu Trinity are described in this verse. Brahma, as the creator represents compassion and is full of knowledge and holds no weapons. Energized activity is a *rajasic* quality. When compassion is associated with action, it brings forth the beauty of creation.

Hari, otherwise known as Vishnu, is the symbol of purity. The *sattvic* quality is forever pure. Spirituality can only sprout in the purest mind. In order to sustain and preserve creation, love and purity are essential.

Rudra represents the fire quality that illumines, burns, and eliminates. Destruction and dissolution are symbolized by fire. Dissolution is necessary for creation to manifest once again. The physical eyes represent the sun and the moon. The third eye, fire, portrays the flame of wisdom; in real wisdom, tranquility manifests as a positive form of inertia, bringing peace, and calmness. Here the state of inactivity is *tamas*.

Verse 84

ekaṃ bhūtaṃ parambrahma
jagat sarva carācaram
nānā bhāvaṃ mano yasya
tasya muktir na jāyate

Translation

The One Supreme God is present in the animate and

inanimate world. If the mind perceives differences in these, liberation becomes impossible.

Metaphorical Interpretation

The universe is called *jagat*, meaning 'that which is constantly changing and disappearing.' Each animate and inanimate object constitutes the universe, and each is the reflection of God's image.

In the Isha Upanishad, the first mantra declares, *isavasyam jagat sarvam:* "God permeates everywhere."

There is no place, time, or circumstance where God does not pervade. A truly spiritual person sees God in all and describes the Absolute as *parambrahma,* or the Supreme Brahman. The Absolute has two aspects: *saguna* and *nirguna,* 'with' and 'without attributes.' God as the Absolute has no form, qualities, and characteristics. When creation began, it was the manifestation of the Cosmic Being under all names and forms, possessing different qualities.

When seekers are able to discern the gold in every ornament, they dispel ignorance. They attach no more importance to the beauty of the object and its design than to the gold itself.

In the Katha Upanishad (2:1:10), Lord Yama (Lord of death) teaches Nachiketa, *mṛtyoḥ sa mṛtyuṃ āpnoti ya iha nānyeva paśyati:* "One who sees multiplicity, approaches death."

The secret of liberation is to find the presence of God in all and remain in the state of knowledge.

Verse 85

ahaṃ śṛsti ahaṃ kālah
apyahaṃ brahmāpyahaṃ harih
ahaṃ rudrāpyahaṃ śunyam
ahaṃ vāpi nirañjanam

Translation

I am Creation, I am Time, I am Brahma, I am Hari, I am Rudra and I am Sunya (vacuum or space). I am Niranjana (Colourless and Formless).

Metaphorical Interpretation

This verse continues and re-emphasizes the foregoing argument. I am Creation. Those who see this unison in all aspects of creation become liberated. The Upanishads declare — *sarvam brahmamayam jagat* — or — *ishavasyamidam sarvam:* "The entire universe is God alone." Since God abides everywhere, a spiritual devotee recognizes the truth of God in all and all in God.

Not just objects, but time too is God. I am *Kala — kala* has many meanings: 'that which measures everything,' 'the span of time,' 'the Lord of Death.' Metaphorically, *ka* means 'matter,' 'nature or *guna'* or 'delusion'; whereas *la* is 'dissolution' or 'disappearance' (*laya).* In this context, *kala* is 'the state of freedom from the delusive power of *maya.' Mahakala* is another name of Shiva, who is the Lord of Time.

I am Brahman*:* is a reinforcement of the *mahavakya,* or the great commandment of the Upanishads — *aham brahmasmi.* Brahman means 'Supreme' or 'the Absolute,' possessing greatness beyond all attributes.

I am Hari: Hari, another name for Vishnu, in scriptures is explained as, *hari harati papani:* "Hari takes away all sins of a devotee."

Hari is metaphorically described in scriptures as,

hakāra pingala varṇa
sarva varna varottama
rakāra teja varṇasyāt
ikāra śakti dāyakah

Hakara, which means the syllable *ha*, illustrates a molten copper colour (which is considered a superior colour), *rakara* or the syllable *ra* depicts its brilliance, and *ikara* or the syllable *i* connotes bestowal of energy. In meditation a seeker experiences many types of colours. To experience union and the formless stage during meditation is to be in Hari.

I am Rudra — Rudra is another name for Lord Shiva, but in this context it stands for *prana,* the principle of life in every living being. In every breath, the vital air or *prana* is circulating in the body, creating an inner vibration experienced during meditation.

I am Sunya (vacuum or space) and Niranjana (colourless and formless). During the process of creation, the vacuum — formless space — was the source from which all other elements: air, fire, water, and earth, emerged. In essence, Sunya refers to the role as 'Father' of creation. Here Sunya also represents the cosmic sound, the primordial sound that is heard during meditation. Such statements are the product of deep meditation, not an intellectual theory.

Verse 86

ahaṃ sarvātmako devi
niṣkāmo gaganopamāh
svabhāva nirmalaṃ śāntam
sa evāhaṃ na samśayah

Translation

O Devi, I am the Soul in everyone, without desires, pure and tranquil, all-pervading like the sky. There is no doubt about this.

Metaphorical Interpretation

I am the Soul in everyone — within the Vedic scriptures it is stated, *sarvatmake brahmani purnarupe:* "I am the soul, the Brahman in all, in my completeness." Each individual or embodied being has a soul, and that soul is essentially divine; it is otherwise known as Shiva. The soul's energy is always pure, never tainted or polluted.

I am free from all desires — desires become the shackles of bondage. When individuals are submerged in a state of ignorance, they suffer from a flood of desires stemming from the mind. The mind, harnessing the sense-organs, wishes to enjoy and possess countless objects. The soul, however, is ever pure and free. The body and the mind are prone to agitation and restlessness, but the soul remains permanently in a state of peaceful bliss.

I am all-pervading like the sky. The space enclosed between the walls and the roof gives an impression of the existence of a room, but when the walls are removed, it becomes open space again or the sky. Likewise, the soul in the body is like the space inside the walls, in reality it was always part of the infinite sky. A body has gross, astral, and causal walls; and these sheaths can be removed through Self-realization, a way to experience formlessness. The nature of the Soul is existence, consciousness, and bliss.

Verse 87

jitendriyo bhavet suro
brahmacārī supaṇḍitah
satyavādi bhaved bhaktah
dātā dhīro ḥite ratah

Translation

He is the real hero, who having victory over the senses is *brahmachari* (celibate), *supandita* (a man of wisdom),

***satyavadi* (truthful), *bhakta* (devoted), *data* (charitable), and *dhira* (calm).**

Metaphorical Interpretation

Sura — is a 'hero' who has achieved thorough control over the restless senses. In both the Upanishads and the Bhagavad Gita, the senses are described as turbulent horses that agitate the mind. The senses, if used correctly, are not really obstacles. Once the mind has been tempered and the senses given proper use, they can become fine instruments to promote spiritual evolution. Mastery over the senses can be gained through discipline and self-control.

Brahmachari — is a seeker whose mind is always engrossed in Brahman, God. The intellect is the vehicle that allows the spiritual aspirant to reach the state of wisdom. The term used in this verse is *supandita. Pandita* is a scholar of the scriptures or a theologian. *Supandita* is a person whose knowledge is not limited to books but to a deeper understanding of life. *Supandita* is a man rich in wisdom and Self-knowledge.

Satyavadi — refers to a highly evolved person, who never flinches from truth. In the Yoga Shastras, there is an elaborate description of being established in truth — "speak truth, speak it sweetly, and speak it with love." A truthful person is full of devotion. God has blessed every individual with many talents, which must be used not only for enjoyment and pleasure but also for the good of others.

Dhira — literally means 'calm and quiet.' *Dhi* stands for 'intellect' and *ra* is translated as 'fire' or 'wisdom.' *Dhira* is a seeker, whose intellect is saturated in knowledge. Such persons are never agitated, or aggressive, instead they are immersed in a permanent state of tranquility and love.

Verse 88

brahmacaryaṃ tapomūlam
dharmamulaṃ dayāsmṛtā
satyavādi bhavet bhaktah
dayā dharmaṃ samācaret

Translation

The root (basis) of *tapa* is *brahmacharya* (celibacy), the basis of dharma **is *daya* (compassion) and *satyavadi* (truthfulness) is the basis of devotion. Follow the path of compassion and righteousness.**

Metaphorical Interpretation

Brahmacharya taporulam — the foundation stone of spiritual life is discipline and self-control. *Brahmacharya* also means 'continence and abstinence from excessive indulgence.' *Tapa* means 'penance,' 'austerity,' and also 'conscious breathing.' The root of spirituality is to be conscious, in every breath, of the presence of God inside and outside, becoming free from the pull of emotion and ego.

Dharma is ordinarily translated as 'religious.' Dharma is not necessarily only a religious concept of moral duty or universal law, but the basic principle that upholds life. *Daya* alludes to transmitting love and being compassionate. In this context, *dharmamulam dayasmrta* means 'being true to one's own Self.' Spiritual seekers should have self-control over their nature and be able to manifest love and compassion in every action.

In spiritual terms, there is nothing greater than compassion and nothing worse than anger. Thus, through calm and conscious breathing, a sincere seeker should avoid anger and dwell in a state filled with love and devotion for God and God's entire creation. This is the true spirit of dharma. It is also Reality, Truth, Brahman. Truthfulness in life is the practical art of spiritual life.

Verse 89

devī uvāca
yogeśvara jagannātha
umāyāḥ prāṇa vallabha
veda sandhyā tapo dhyānam
homakarma kulaṃ katham

Translation

Devi said, "O Yogeshwara, Jagannatha, beloved of Uma, what are the Veda*(s), sandhya(s)* (evening rituals), *tapa(s)* (penance), *dhyanam* (meditation), *homa karma* (fire rituals), and *kulam* (energy)."

Metaphorical Interpretation

In this verse, Parvati addresses Lord Shiva with meaningful names that carry a special significance:

Yogeshwara — means 'Lord or Master of Yoga.' A true yogi is a befitting teacher who explains the meaning of life and the symbolic content of the scriptures.

Jagannatha — can be broken into two words — *natha* means 'Lord,' 'master,' or 'husband'; *jagat* means 'the changing universe' or 'nature.' Essentially, the allegorical meaning is that the Lord of the universe is beyond changes, even though the nature of the universe is to constantly evolve.

Umayah prana vallabha — means literally 'beloved to Uma as her breath.' Uma is another name for Parvati: It is no coincidence that Uma and *Om* have the same origin. *Om* consists of three syllables *a u m,* and Uma also consists of the same letters *u m a. Om* symbolizes Purusha or God and Uma represents *prakriti* or Mother Nature.

Parvati then asks about various scriptures as well as rituals, and mantras obligatory for an individual.

As mentioned before, the Vedas are considered humankind's ancient treatises on wisdom, classified into four scriptures: Rig, Yajur, Sama, and Atharva. Each Veda consists of a mixture between ceremonial rituals and spiritual wisdom, otherwise known as Upanishads or Vedanta. In Sanskrit, Veda is derived from the root word *vid,* 'to know,' an aptitude inherent to each individual. Since the ultimate form of knowledge is Self-knowledge, the Vedas indicate the path, the means to achieve the goal of Self-realization.

Sandhya — has a variety of meanings: on a primary level, *sandhya* is 'evening,' derived from the root-word *sandhi* or 'junction of time.' There are three junctions of time — early morning, noon, and evening — these are known as *trisandhya* or three propitious times for ritualistic practices. Metaphorically, *sandhya* can be interpreted as 'balance' — a state of balance between the mind and the breath. Allegorically, *sandhya* can be linked to *samyak dhyana* or perfect meditation during the three junctions of time.

Tapa — is defined as 'austerities' or 'penance' undertaken by a mendicant, in order to fortify spiritual life and achieve perfection. *Tapa* can also mean 'sacrificial practices' in order to achieve *siddhis* or occult powers. Metaphorically, *tapa* symbolizes conscious breathing and directing the mind towards the highest goal.

Dhyana — literally means 'meditation.' The word is derived from the root *dhi* 'intellect.' Meditation is to direct the intellect consciously towards the goal of Self-realization. *Dhyana* can also be interpreted as a meditative examination of Truth.

Homa — is a ritualistic fire ceremony offering an oblation of ghee and other materials into the holy fire, a ritual often accompanied by specific prayers or mantras.

Kulam — means 'energy' hidden in each individual. But in spite of its tremendous potential, this energy lies untapped.

Through the practice of self-discipline, a seeker can utilize energy to achieve the highest purpose of life.

Verse 90

īśvara uvāca
aśvamedha sahasrāṇi
vājapeya śatāni ca
brahmajñānaṃ samaṃ puṇyam
kaḷāṃ nārhanti ṣoḍaśīm

Translation

Ishwara said, "Compared to the greatness (derived from) knowledge of Brahman, the virtue earned by performing a thousand *ashvamedhas* and a hundred *vajapeyas,* is only equal to one sixteenth of it."

Metaphorical Interpretation

In this verse, Lord Shiva speaks of the completeness of Self-knowledge or the knowledge of Brahman. Self-knowledge is the yogi's supreme attainment, and can only be achieved through self-discipline and sincere contemplation.

In ancient times, highly evolved persons, sages, or emperors, who achieved unparalleled success in their lives, performed Vedic rituals called *yajnas* or sacrifices to glorify the state of union with Brahman. These *yajnas:*

i) *Ashvamedha yajna,*
ii) *Vajapeya yajna,*

are described in the Ahsvamedhika Parva, Bhagavatam (3:12:40), and in the Mahabharata.

Ashvamedha yajna literally means 'horse sacrifice.' This special ritual was performed to establish the supremacy of a powerful ruler over other kings. Such *yajna* involved years of arduous preparation and elaborate ritualistic performance. But on spiritual and metaphorical level, *ashva* refers to 'the senses' and *medha* 'to slay' or 'to offer.' *Ashvamedha* means to control the senses, offering each one to God and behold God through it.

Ashva can be interpreted as 'restlessness.' *Ashvamedha*, in figurative terms, means to sacrifice restlessness in order to experience calmness. *Ashva* also indicates the number 'seven' and symbolically represents the seven chakras. So *ashvamedha* has been interpreted as the offering of the seven chakras to God, remaining in God-consciousness.

Linguistically, *ashvamedha* can be broken into two components: *a* means 'not'; *shva* means 'tomorrow.' It teaches the spiritual aspirant not to postpone until tomorrow what can be done today. A seeker, who utilizes time intelligently to reach the goal, is blessed with divine grace.

Vajapeya yajna literally means 'to drink water' —*vajam* is 'water'; *peya* is 'to drink.' Metaphorically, *vajapeya yajna* signifies to bring inner purity and love into everyday life. The goal of such practices is to acquire knowledge of Brahman.

In this verse Shiva emphasizes the superiority of the knowledge of Brahman over multiple traditional sacrifices. Divine wisdom is the greatest achievement.

Verse 91

sarvadā sarva tīrtheṣu
tat phalaṃ labhate śuciḥ
brahmajñānaṃ samaṃ puṇyam
kaḷāṃ nārhanti ṣoḍaśīm

Translation

Compared to the knowledge of Brahman, the virtue earned by constantly going on pilgrimages to all the holy places is only equal to one of the sixteen *kalas* (parts).

Metaphorical Interpretation

Going on pilgrimages to the four corners of India is an important part of Hindu tradition. Those who can afford, do it to collect merit. In this verse Shiva, once again, states the importance of the knowledge of Brahman, establishing its superiority over the merit gathered by pilgrimages.

In the Skanda Purana, there is a beautiful description of the holy places of pilgrimage,

satya tīrthaṃ kṣamā tīrthaṃ tīrthaṃ indriya nigahah
sarva bhūta dayā tīrthaṃ tīrthānāṃ satyavādinā
jñāna tīrthaṃ tapas tīrthaṃ kathitaṃ saptathīrthakam

"Truthfulness, forgiveness, sense-control, compassion for all beings, knowledge, and austerity are known as the seven *teerthas* (holy places of pilgrimage). People go on pilgrimages to attain spiritual merits and purify the mind. A real pilgrimage is to experience inner peace and love. Through the cultivation of virtues and the practice of meditation, a seeker gets realization."

A crucial element on the search for Self-knowledge is *suchi* or purity. In the Katha Upanishad, purity is described in the following way — One who knows the Self is really pure. The highest feat in life is the attainment of *Brahmajñana* or 'knowledge of the Absolute.' In this state, existence becomes an unbroken flow of peace, love, and bliss.

Verse 92

na mitraṃ na ca putraś ca
na pitā na ca vāndhavāh
na svāmi na gurostulyam
yaddṛṣṭaṃ paramampadam

Translation

Friend, son, father, relative, or husband, none is equal to the guru, who has realization of the Absolute.

Metaphorical Interpretation

In spiritual life, the need for an enlightened guide, to show the way is essential. Nothing in the world can be compared to the guru-disciple relationship, which is eternal. When spiritual aspirants have implicit faith, love, loyalty, and devotion for the guru, they are already pointed towards Self-realization. The real guru, however, is the soul within.

A caring guru has multiple roles:

– The guru is *mitra* or 'friend' because he always stands firm in the hour of need, showering his love and affection;

– The guru is *putra* or 'son' because he protects the weak from downfall. In spiritual terms a guru helps his disciples to become free from sins and suffering;

– The guru is *pita* or father because he disciplines his children with love. A successful guide keeps his offsprings on the right track, by making them conscious of their duty;

– The guru is a *bandhava* or 'close relative' because he helps to free his kin from *bandhana* or bondage;

– The guru is a *swami,* 'Lord' or 'husband,' because he constantly gives his care, love, guidance, and support. A guru's devotion and compassion are limitless.

Scriptural or theoretical knowledge is not enough to be a realized guru. He needs to have the direct experience of Truth.

A guru is — *yad drshtam paramam padam* — 'one who has realized the feet of the Lord' (achieved the goal of life).

Verse 93

na ca vidyā gurostulyam
na tīrthaṃ na ca devatāh
gurostulya na vai ko'pi
yaddṛṣṭaṃ paramampadam

Translation

There is no *vidya* (knowledge), no holy place or any gods equal to the guru, who has realization of the Absolute.

Metaphorical Interpretation

This verse elaborates further on the distinct role of the guru, comparing him to *vidya (*knowledge), *teertham* (holy places), and even *devata* (gods). The guru possesses a storehouse of wisdom enabling him to steer a disciple towards a higher level of spiritual experience. The guru personifies God's love and wisdom. A devoted disciple who follows the guru's instructions incorporating them in daily life, will reap more benefits than by visiting all the holy places.

In the Guru Gita it is said,

gururbrahmā gururvisnur gururdevo mahesvarah
guruḥ sākṣāt parambrahma tasmai śri gurave namah

"The guru is Brahma, the guru is Vishnu, the guru is Shiva, and the guru is Parabrahma, the Supreme Lord. I bow to the guru.".

Verse 94

ekamapyāksharaṃ yastu
guruḥ śiṣyāt prabhodhayet
pṛthīvyāṃ nāsti tat dravyam
yat dattvā arṇīṃ bhavet

Translation

(Even the) Knowledge of one letter imparted to the *sishya* (disciple) by the guru (teacher, divine master) is invaluable, and there is nothing in the whole world that can repay this debt.

Metaphorical Interpretation

The guru is the mouthpiece of spiritual wisdom, which he transmits to a befitting student. Sincere disciples, who are ready to transform their life through self-discipline and dedicated service, will gain unlimited spiritual treasure.

As we grow up in the world, we learn many things from countless different sources; parents, brothers and sisters, children, friends, teachers, and even from nature itself. We are indebted by the most insignificant morsel, for even just one letter is crucial to incrementing our understanding.

Another meaning of *ekamapyakshara* — even one letter — is described in the Gita (8:19), "The single syllable *Om* is the source of all knowledge, and the symbol of God."

Within all yogic and tantric practices, the guru teaches his disciples to understand the significance of the primordial sound *Om* and to listen to it continuously, while immersed in deep meditation. This sacred syllable bestows immense calmness and opens the door to God-realization. The illuminated master awakens the consciousness of his students, by igniting the spark of spirituality within. This knowledge brings understanding eventually transforming it into wisdom. Such endowment forms a permanent bond between the guru and the disciple. It is an un-repayable debt.

In the scriptures, there is a description of five types of debts that each individual should strive to repay:

Deva runa	debt to God,
Rshi runa	debt to the masters,
Pitru runa	debt to the parents,
Nru runa	debt to humanity,
Bhuta runa	debt to creation as a whole.

Five offerings or activities help to redeem such debt:

Deva yajna	Offering oblations to God,
Brahma yajna	Imparting spiritual knowledge to worthy seekers,
Pitru yajna	Rendering tribute to departed family members,
Nru yajna athiti seva	Serving the needs of our fellow human beings,
Bhuta yajna	Preserving ecological balance by protecting animals and the environment.

It is harder to repay the immense debt that disciples have with their guru than any of those listed above. If a dedicated disciple reaches the goal of Self-realization, the debt to the guru actually increases. Service to God and gurus must always be performed with the utmost humility and love.

Verse 95

yasya kasya na dātavyam
brahmajñānaṃ sugopitam
yasya kasyāpi bhaktasya
sadgurustasya dīyate

Translation

The well-kept secret knowledge of Brahman should not be given to undeserving people. This should be imparted by the *Sadguru* only to one who shows real devotion.

Metaphorical Interpretation

A guru has a duty to maintain the sacrosanct nature of the knowledge he hands down to posterity. Spiritual knowledge must be revealed only to trustworthy disciples. In Vedantic texts, there is a description of *adhikari* or the 'qualified disciple.'

A sincere student must possess the following qualities:

Viveka	discrimination,
Vairagya	non-attachment,
Shama	equanimity of mind,
Dama	control over the senses,
Uparati	desire for growth or evolution,
Titiksha	forbearance or tolerance,
Shraddha	faith and love in the teaching of the guru and the holy scriptures,
Samadhana	contemplative outlook,
Mumukshutva	desire for liberation.

Lord Shiva dictates, *brahmavidya sugopitam:* "Keep spiritual knowledge free from abuse and adulteration." In other words, such precious gift should be kept hidden. Knowledge in the hands of an unfit person is as dangerous as a scientific discovery in the hands of a ruthless individual, or fire in the hands of a child. A worthy disciple is rare to find; one must be loyal, sincere, devoted, faithful, and selfless.

Verse 96

mantra pujā tapodhyānam
homaṃ japaṃ balikriyām
sannyāsaṃ sarva karmāṇi
laukikāni tyajet budhah

Translation

All the traditional rituals like mantra (chanting), *puja* (worship), *tapa* (penance), *dhyanam* (study), *homam* (fire ceremony), *japam* (chanting), *bali kriyam* (the act of sacrifice), and *sannyasam* (renunciation), are given up by the one who is really wise.

Metaphorical Interpretation

In this verse, Lord Shiva refers to the most frequent rituals undertaken as a daily routine and are the foundation of spiritual life. But as the devotee evolves in the quest of truth, these observances lose their poignancy leaving room for a much deeper communion with the Absolute.

The definition of such practices is the following:

i) *Mantra — mananat trayate iti:* "That which helps in liberation through contemplation." Mantra is a sacred formula or prayer chanted overtly or silently. To be effective, a mantra has to be properly transmitted by the guru.

ii) *Puja* — is derived from the word *puj* 'to worship,' 'to adore,' or 'to bow.' *Puja* is a form of ritualistic worship requiring flowers, fruits, and so on. *Puja* can be external or mental. In order to perform mental ritualistic worship, a focused mind is essential, rendering other articles and utensils useless.

iii) *Tapa* — means 'penance' or 'austerity.' The ability to sacrifice or mortify the body in a certain way brings discipline and sense-control.

iv) *Dhyana* — is 'meditation.' There are two types; *saguna dhyana* (meditation on a form) and *nirguna dhyana* (meditation on the formless).

v) *Homa* — is 'a ritualistic oblation into a ceremonial fire,' which is performed with the proper chanting of mantras.

vi) *Japa* — is 'chanting' either overtly or silently.

vii) *Bali kriya* — is 'sacrifice.' As an external form of worship, devotees offer fruits or animals. In inner worship, a spiritual seeker destroys the inner animal qualities, such as anger, jealousy, and pride.

viii) *Sannyas* — is the renunciation of worldly activities andpossessions.

Devotees who have attained absolute wisdom become free from all traditional rituals, because they live in a state of inner awakening. A truly spiritual person is liberated and enlightened and is known as *buddha,* 'the incarnation of wisdom.' As one reaches the destination, the means of conveyance, or outer accruements, are no longer useful.

Verse 97

samsargāt vahavo doṡāh
niḥsaṅgāt vahavo guṇāh
tasmāt sarva prayatnena
yatiḥ sangaṃ parityajet

Translation

Vices are accumulated through association with others. Non-attachment promotes good qualities. So by every effort, and through self-control, one should give up all company.

Metaphorical Interpretation

In the same way that clothes get dirty, the mind becomes polluted in the company of evil-minded people. The person is known by the company one keeps. For a spiritual aspirant, bad company makes it easier to fall into the grasp of vices, whereas good company helps the best qualities within and keeps the mind engrossed in elevated thoughts. Such company protects the mind from the lure of the senses.

Thus Acharya Shankara describes the benefit of good company,

satsangatve nissangatvam
nissangatve nirmohatvam
nirmohatve nischala tattvam
nischala tattve jivanmuktih

"Good company encourages detachment. Detachment frees one from delusion. Freed from delusion, one achieves steadiness to experience Truth. Such an experience liberates one while still alive."

Association with bad company breeds many vices; one can learn much wickedness from the company of others. A sincere seeker should try to live completely detached. By living alone and secluded the spiritual aspirant can progress on the road to self-improvement. The Bhagavad Gita teaches, *aratir jana samsadi:* "Feel no attraction for public gatherings." The true renunciate or *yati* should try, in every possible way, to be free from social activity. *Yati* is defined as *samyatayati iti,* 'one who tries to discipline life.'

Metaphorically, a devotee should try to avoid any association that distracts the sense organs, and enter into the cave of the cranium or the *sahasrara chakra,* to experience seclusion, and taste perennial bliss.

Verse 98

akāraḥ sātviko jñeya
ukāro rājasaḥ smṛtah
makārastāmasaḥ proktah
tribhiḥ prakṛtirucyate

Translation

In *aum,* the letter *a* represents *sattva, u* represents *rajas* and *m* represents *tamas,* which are the three qualities of nature.

Metaphorical Interpretation

This verse explains the sacred syllable *Om* (*a u m*) as a combination of the three modes of nature. Nature or *prakriti* can be of three types: *sattvic* (calm), *rajasic* (restless), and *tamasic* (idle). When these three modes of nature are in balance, creation or change ceases. The dance of nature begins when there is imbalance in these three qualities. The predominance of the *sattvic* factor brings calmness, peace, and pure happiness. The *rajasic* factor brings forth more activity, effort, endeavour, and achievement. The *tamàsic* factor is evident in laziness, lethargy, sleep, or inertia.

Om consists of three syllables: *a u m* and these three represent *sattva, rajas,* and *tamas,* respectively; *a* is the first syllable in the Sanskrit alphabet, representing 'God' and 'Creation'; *u* is the fifth vowel, representing 'progressive existence,' and *m* is the last of the fifth group of consonants, representing 'knowledge in five chakras.'

The Play of *Prakriti*

SOUND	PRAKRITI/ PURUSHA	VEDAS	LOKAS/ LORD	4 EXISTENCES	COLOURS
A	sattva	rik	bhuh	prithivi (earth)	pita (yellow)
U	rajas	yajur	bhuva	antariksha (inner space)	vidyut (golden yellow)
M	tamas	sama	svah	savita (sun)	shukla(white)
AUM	purusha (indwelling Self)	atharva	atma (soul)	dhruva (pole star)	colourless

Verse 99

akṣarā prakṛti proktā
akṣaraḥ svayaṃ iśvarah
īśvarānirgatā sāhi
prakṛtirguṇavandhanā

Translation

The *akshara* (alphabet) is *prakriti* (nature), *akshara* (imperishable), and Ishwara. From Ishwara (God) comes *prakriti* (nature), who is associated with the three qualities.

Metaphorical Interpretation

In the Bhagavad Gita (15:16) there is a beautiful description of *kshara, akshara,* and *purushottama. Kshara* consists of two parts: *ksha* and *ra. Ksha* means 'that which undergoes modification and changes,' *ra* is the root word for 'fire.' *Kshara* therefore means 'perishable.' The prefix '*a*' indicates negation: *a + kshara* means 'imperishable.'

The fire element in each letter of the alphabet, has the power to burn or to illuminate. Words can burn ignorance and remove darkness. They can also bring pain if they are not used properly, since fire's nature is to burn. Since each letter or *akshara* has the ability to bring knowledge and understanding, sacred knowledge is imperishable.

Kshara or 'perishable' is *prakriti. Prakriti* symbolizes 'creation,' 'the material world,' 'the psychological field within the body,' and 'the lower chakras.' *Akshara* is Ishwara or Lord Shiva, who is by nature imperishable. The Bhagavad Gita declares that *kutastha*, the place between the eyebrows (*ajna chakra),* represents the place of *akshara,* the immutable. From Ishwara (*atma*) comes the manifestation of the material world, from the *ajna chakra* descend the five lower chakras.

Taittiriya Upanishad teaches, *etasmat atmano akasha sambhuta:* "From the Self (Absolute) came space."

Prakriti symbolizes Mother Nature composed of *triguna* or the three modes of nature. If devotees remain below the *ajna chakra,* they will become engrossed in the material world and forget divinity manifested within. If spiritual aspirants concentrate in the *ajna chakra* or *sahasrara chakra,* they can achieve the state of liberation and complete oneness with the Absolute.

Verse 100

sā māyā pālini śaktih
sṛṣti samhāra kāriṇī
avidyā mohinī yā sā
sabdarupā yaśasvinī

Translation

O *Yashasvini* (Glorious One), *maya* is the *palini shakti* (nourishing and preserving energy), the cause of *srishti* (creation) and *samhara* (dissolution), and it is also ignorance and delusion. (Yet, the same) *maya* manifests as the divine sound.

Metaphorical Interpretation

Maya is the basis of creation, sustenance, and dissolution. *Maya* is often considered as both the delusive and illusive power of nature, depending on the seeker's level of enlightenment. But, *maya* can also be understood as *ma* (the Divine Mother) and *ya* (existence). In other words, it is the play of the Divine Mother.

Maya is the understated energy in living beings. *Maya* creates, upholds and is the cause of play and pleasure throughout creation. *Maya* is sometimes correlated to *avidya,* which is defined as 'ignorance' or 'lack of knowledge.' At other times, *maya* is 'desire' or 'passion' known as *kama.* This is a reflection of the *rajasic* quality of nature. *Maya* has also been interpreted as *mohini* which means 'puzzle,' 'delusion,' or 'infatuation.' Therefore, *maya* is the power that creates confusion. This corresponds to the *tamasic* quality of nature.

At a different level the most fundamental manifestation of *maya*, and the core of its illusive power, appears when the seeker is immersed in deep meditation, totally engrossed in a peaceful state of mind. At this point, *maya* comes in the shape of the divine sound. It is by listening to this primordial echo, linking a devotee to God, that a state of inner tranquility is reached. This is otherwise known as the *sattvic* state of mind.

MAYA	DEVI	MODE OF NATURE	STATE OF MIND	NAMES	STATE	
Sattva	Vaishnavi	Peace	Calm	Shabdarupa	Sthiti (Sound)	(Creation)
Rajas	Brahmani	Activity	Restless	Palini Shakti	Shristi (Protective)	(Sustenance)
Tamas	Shivani	Delusion	Lazy	Mohini	Samhara (Illusive)	(Dissolution)

This is described in the yogic scriptures,

dhvanirantargataṃ jyoti
jyotirantargataṃ manah
tanmanovilayaṃ yāti
tad viṣno paramampadam

"When one goes deep into sound, (one) experiences light within. Within the light, the mind becomes purified. That pure mind dissolves at the Supreme Feet of the Lord."

Verse 101

akārascaiva ṛkveda
ukāra yajurucyate
makāra sāmavedastu
triṣuyuktā pyatharvaṇah

Translation

The letter *a* is Rig Veda, *u* is Yajur Veda, and *m* is Sama Veda. All three together (*aum*) make the Atharvana Veda.

Metaphorical Interpretation

Earlier *Om* is defined as *akshara purusha*, or the imperishable

Soul within the body, the manifestation of Brahman within the universe.

On another level *Om* is the primordial echo — the root of creation, sustenance, dissolution, and ultimately liberation. All knowledge: *para* and *apara,* manifests itself from this sound. *Om* is the continuous divine vibration consisting of the three syllables *a u m.* This sacred resonance encompasses different steps of evolution and spiritual experience.

The universality and all pervasiveness of *Om* is further emphasized here in this verse. *Om* is the source of the four Vedas; *a* symbolizes the Rig Veda (or the path of knowledge through speech); *u* represents the Yajur Veda (or the path of union that brings emancipation); *m* is the Sama Veda (or the path of harmony); *a u m* put together becomes the Atharva Veda (or the path of happiness and bliss).

Verse 102

omkārastu pluto jñeyah
trināda iti sajñitaḥ
akārastvatha bhūrloka
ukāro bhuvarucyate

Translation

Omkara is full to the brim with these three sounds: _a_ represents the _bhur loka_ (the earth) and _u_ the _bhuvar loka_ (the subtle world).

Metaphorical Interpretation

Not only the complete compendium of knowledge, the four Vedas, *Om* envelops the creation process and the cosmos. *Om* is the divine vibration that can be heard in deep meditation and contemplation: the omnipresent sound irrespective of time, place, and causation. This eternal and continuous resonance fills the heart with divine love, and the mind and intellect with divine wisdom.

The *lokas* are the regions or levels of existence of living beings in any given world. In this verse, Lord Shiva describes how the *Om* sound pervades everywhere: *a* represents *bhur loka* or the physical level and *u* represents *bhuvar loka* or the subtle world. In the Gayatri Mantra, there is a description of *bhur, bhuvah,* and *svah loka*, or the three planes of existence. The highest of the three regions is the *svah loka* and it is considered to be a heavenly world. In this verse, Lord Shiva only mentions the two vowels: *a* and *u, m* the consonant is mentioned in the next verse.

Verse 103

savyanjanaṃ akārastu
svarlokastu vidhīyate
akṣaraiḥ tribhiretaiśca
bhavet ātmā vyavasthita

Translation

The consonant *m* represents the *svah loka.* The soul is manifested in these three letters.

Metaphorical Interpretation

M in Sanskrit is not only a consonant but it represents all the twenty-five types of consonants from *ka* up to *ma.* Speech, words or thoughts are nothing but a combination of consonants and vowels. However, when a seeker meditates on the source of all sounds (*Om* or *Aum*), all thoughts and mind disappear, and the meditator becomes focused in one sound and merges in the state of superconsciousness or the cosmic conscious state.

At this higher level of consciousness, the spiritual aspirant transcends the seven planes of existence within the seven chakras, and ultimately becomes established in the Self, in the *sahasrara chakra* or the crown of the head. This is known as *atma-vyavasthiti*, or 'the state of complete establishment in the Self.'

Verse 104

akāraḥ pṛthivī jñeyā
pīta varṇena samyutāh
antarīkṣaṃ ukārastu
vidyutvarṇa ihocyate

Translation

Know that the letter *a* is the earth which is yellow in colour, (and) the letter *u* is the *antariksha* (the inner sky) which has the colour of lightning.

Metaphorical Interpretation

In this verse, Lord Shiva teaches that by penetrating the chakras to flow upwards into the inner space, the meditator will be able to experience divine illumination. The *muladhara chakra* is the place of the earth element, which flashes a yellow coloured light representing the letter *a*. With the practice of a yogic technique, such as Kriya Yoga, the spiritual seeker concentrates on the inner space, in the cavity of the cranium, and internally sees the brilliance of light made up of different colours, ascending from the lower chakras. When *antariksha* (the inner sky) is reached, representing the letter *u,* the seeker experiences a reddish bright light. In yogic language this is known as 'the soul-fire.'

Verse 105

makār svariti jñeyah
śuklavarṇena samyutah
dhruvam ekākṣaraṃ brahma
omityevaṃ vyavasthitam

Translation

Know that the letter *m* is *svar loka* (which is) white in colour. Brahman is decidedly *a u m,* in which everything is present.

Metaphorical Interpretation

As spiritual seekers enter deeper into meditation, reaching the heavenly blissful state, they see all traces of coloured light dissolving into a white haze. This is *m* or *svar loka* known as the heavenly world. At this point sincere devotees experience divine light, divine sound, and the cessation of all thoughts. This is the state of *dhruva* or 'steadiness in the north.' *Dhruva* symbolizes the polestar, alluding to the fact that a seeker must search the extreme north in the inner sky to become merged in *akshara Brahman.*

In the Bhagavad Gita (8:13), Lord Krishna teaches, *om iti ekākṣaraṃ brahma:* "This is the state when one is completely free from body consciousness and merges in divine love."

Verse 106

devī uvāca
sthūlasya lakṣaṇam vṛhi
kathaṃ mano vilīyate
paramārthaṃ ca nirvāṇam
sthūla sūkṣmasya lakṣaṇam

Translation

Devi said, "What are the qualities of the gross body; how does the mind become dissolved? Also tell me about *paramartham* (the supreme goal), nirvana (liberation), and the qualities of gross and subtle."

Metaphorical Interpretation

In this verse, Parvati asks Lord Shiva the last set of questions, pertaining to the following subjects:

i) The qualities of the gross body,
ii) The dissolution of the subtle body (mind),
iii) The supreme goal of life,
iv) Nirvana, or the ultimate state of liberation.

Each soul is enclosed in three layers of existence: physical, subtle or astral, and causal. Through proper understanding and disciplined practice, seekers manage to make progress on the spiritual path and are able to discard attachment to the physical and astral bodies. Thus, they reach liberation.

Ordinary people remain engrossed in the body and in the material world, slaves to the sense organs. The purpose of life is not *artha* (material possession) or *kama* (pleasure through enjoyment); the supreme goal of life (*paramartha*) is nirvana or liberation. This waveless state implies the cessation of all thought, in order to reach complete communion with God.

Verse 107

īśvara uvāca
yena jñanena he devi
vidyate na ca kilviṣī
pṛthivyapastathā tejo
vāyurākāśameva ca

Translation

Ishwara said, "By this knowledge, O Devi, one is free from all sins and the elements like earth, water, fire, air, and ether."

Metaphorical Interpretation

In this verse, Lord Shiva glorifies supreme knowledge. Ignorance leads to repeated mistakes, a life of misery and bondage tied to the chain of birth and rebirth. Knowledge removes the darkness of ignorance granting liberation as well as immortality. Knowledge bestows freedom from sins and suffering; it is the fire that burns up all the seeds of karma.

Human beings contain earth, water, fire (sun), air, and sky, the same elements that constitute the external world. These five elements are also present, in a subtle way, in the five spinal centers (chakras). By the inner purification of the mind, and through persistent self-effort and the divine grace of the guru, spiritual seekers are able to experience Truth.

Verse 108

sthula rūpī sthito 'yamca
sukṣmaṃ ca anyathāsthita

Translation

One who is in the *sthula rupa* (the gross body), is also in the *sukshma* (the subtle body) and even beyond.

Metaphorical Interpretation

The all-pervading God (Brahman) is present in the gross, astral, and causal worlds, inside and outside. In the process of spiritual evolution, a seeker's consciousness travels to the astral layer. When awareness reaches the causal level, it is merged in the eternal Self. Once this process is culminated, the seeker is saturated in supreme knowledge, and experiences the presence of the Absolute at every instance, in everything. This transformation is known as liberation.

Verse 109

sthirāsano bhavet nityam
cintā-nidrā-vivarjitah
āśu sa jāyate yogī
nānyathā śiva bhāṣitam

Translation

Shiva says there is no other way of becoming a yogi, except by sitting in a firm posture and constantly meditating, devoid of thought(s) or sleep.

Metaphorical Interpretation

In these last two verses Lord Shiva summarizes his final instructions in order to achieve self-evolution.

i) *Sthirasano bhavet* — *sthira* means 'steady' or

'equipoise'; *asana* refers to 'the posture' or 'the seat.' Metaphorically, this means to sit in a fixed posture to meditate for a longer period of time. The regular practice of yoga and meditation brings discipline to the body and the mind. Steadiness in practice is an essential ingredient in reaching Self-realization.

ii) *Nityam* — is 'constant.' Metaphorically, this means to be unwavering by becoming well established in the soul.

iii) *Nidra — vivarjitah* alludes to 'the calmness of the mind before falling asleep.' Sleep is an obstacle to spiritual pursuit; laziness and the excessive need for sleep must be conquered in order to reach the goal. Metaphorically, sleep is the state of ignorance.

iv) Be a yogi — the devotee follows the direct guidance of a qualified guru and becomes a yogi. Only a yogi can achieve emancipation and knowledge. This is the true meaning of Self-realization.

Verse 110

ya idaṃ paṭhate nityam
śṛṇvati ca dine dine
sarva pāpa viśuddhātmā
śivalokaṃ sa gacchati

Translation

One who reads or listens to this every day, will be freed from all sins, becoming pure and attaining *shiva loka* (the abode of Shiva).

Metaphorical Interpretation

Every holy book in Hinduism begins with a prayer and ends

with the glorification of the scriptures known as *phala sruti*. Holy books should be assimilated, understood, and put into daily practice, but theoretical erudition is not enough. Sincere aspirants must be free from all impurities to be able to merge in God-consciousness.

This is the path to reach *shiva loka* or climb Mount Kailasha, hidden amid the internal snow-peaked Himalayas. Once divine energy is manifested, all propensities of the mind dissolve and the purpose of life is complete.

Through self-discipline, immersed in deep meditation, seekers enter the state of superconsciousness, or perfect union with the Absolute. A pure mind is the abode of God.

om brahmarpanamastu

Let this work be offered to God

Epilogue

There is a symbiotic relationship between life and learning. Life is an opportunity to learn; and real learning consists of mastering the art of living. Different spiritual traditions encourage discipline to attain the ultimate purpose of life: to evolve one's consciousness, to feel peace within. Modern educational system focuses on pragmatic issues of material success, but ignores the quintessential aim of human existence. Most religious traditions, however, pivot around this noble cause.

Yoga and Tantra are such ancient spiritual disciplines intended to instruct seekers on the spiritual path. These sacred teachings have been handed down from time immemorial and are composed of various revered texts of spiritual wisdom with a practical application and implications. Besides imparting thorough theoretical knowledge, the texts focus on practical application enabling seekers to experience the essence.

Jñana Sankalini Tantra is in verse form and consists of a philosophical and esoteric dialogue between Lord Shiva and his consort, Parvati. The divine pair in their love, dedication, and unity also symbolizes the relationship between a master and the disciple, God and the spiritual seeker.

Practice with implicit faith and love is the only way to reach perfection. In order to attain such divine goal of inner transformation a spiritual guide is necessary. The guide's teaching applied to daily life builds a strong foundation and paves the way to ultimate enlightenment.

The Yoga Sutras of Patañjali declares that sincere seekers, full of love and devotion, should practice and follow the instructions of the teacher until they are firmly established in a state of permanent communion with God.

In both Yoga and Tantra, the direct guidance of an inspiring teacher is considered essential to eliminate negative qualities and pointing the way to spiritual enlightenment. Life's goal is to attain and constantly struggle, if necessary, for inner perfection and emancipation.

I was blessed with such a guru. My master, Paramahamsa Hariharanandaji, taught that an ounce of practice was better than a ton of theories. He always maintained that a steady and steadfast practice is a prerequisite for spiritual evolution.

My Guruji, a symbol of love, devotion, and selfless action lived an exemplary life. Under his careful guidance, I studied and meditated on a wide range of spiritual texts. He helped me transform from within as my consciousness evolved.

Gurudev inspired this book and I started writing it in 1997 and it took great effort to bring it in the present form. Although this work could not be published during his physical life, every line is imbued with his divine presence.

I bow to my guru, and to my guru's gurus.

May this work remain a tribute to their teachings.

Prajnanananda

Glossary of Sanskrit Words

Abhyasa	practice
Abhisheka	a form of ritual, in which water, milk and other substances are poured on the deities with mantras. It is also practiced while initiating a disciple into the path of Tantra.
Achara	mode of practice, conduct, discipline
Acharya	master, teacher, a person established in good conduct
Adhikari	qualified disciple
Adhyatma vidya	spiritual wisdom from the scriptures or from the teacher
Adinatha	first guru, usually another name for Shiva
Advaita	state of unity and oneness, a branch of Indian Philosophy
Agama	the supreme knowledge of Shiva taught to Parvati, Tantra
Aghora	no darkness or fear, literally a special tantric practice
Ahamkara	ego, attitude of doership
Ajna chakra	the third eye, in the medulla oblongata, a place of concentration in between the eyebrows
Akarma	actionless
Akasha	space, sky, ether
Akshara	syllable, alphabet, imperishable, soul
Akshara tattva	the philosophy of letters
Akula	Lord Shiva
Allahabad	The name of a city where the three holy rivers, Ganga, Yamuna, and Saraswati meet. It is one of the places where the Kumbhamela takes place every twelve

	years.
Anahata chakra	dorsal or heart center
Anirvachaniya	one that is beyond words, it represents soul, God and even *maya*
Antaratma	inner soul
Antarjyoti	inner light in the crown of the head
Anthariksha	inner sky
Anukalpa	substituted materials
Apa	water element
Apara vidya	material knowledge, material science, worldly experiences
Aparabindu	lower point, the Shiva principle
Aparanada	lower sound or vibration
Aryavarta	another name of the ancient India, the abode of Aryans
Atharvana Vedá	the fourth Veda
Atma	soul, the indwelling spirit
Atma tirtha	seat of the soul
Avidya	ignorance, nescience
Avyakta	the un-manifested *Bhagavad Gita* A spiritual handbook; in the battle of Mahabharata, the scripture of Yoga, dialogue between Shri Krishna and Arjuna
Bhagavatam	A sacred scripture of 18,000 verses written by Sage Vyasa
Bhairava	the attendants of Shiva
Bhakti	devotion, a path of experiencing love for God
Bija	seed
Bindu	point
Brahma	god as creator, the first Lord of the Hindu Trinity
Brahmacharya	abstinence or perpetual celibacy

Brahmagni	divine fire
Brahmajñana	knowledge of the Absolute, highest state of wisdom
Brahman	God, the Ultimate Absolute, the Formless Spirit
Brahmanda	universe in the shape of egg
Brahmashakti	manifested power of God
Caryapada	path of spiritual evolution practiced in Tantra
Chakra	a spiritual center, wheel, disc, energy centers in spine and brain
Cit	consciousness
Dakshinachara	right hand or favorable path, a tantric practice
Damara Tantra	tantric text
Damaru	kettle drum
Darshana	Philosophy, the path of direct experience
Daya	compassion
Deha	the body
Deva	male form of God, the illumined one
Devadeva	the indwelling Self, 'God of all gods'
Devas	gods
Devesha	the Soul, the Lord of gods
Devi	female form of God
Dharma	discipline, divine law
Dharmashastra	scripture of ethics and morality
Dhyana	meditation, contemplation
Dhyanam	study of scriptures
Dik tattva	principle of ten directions
Diksha	spiritual initiation, instruction
Durga	Divine Mother
Dvara	door, entrance
Ganapati/Ganesha	deity of success and wisdom, son of Shiva and Parvati
Ganapatya Tantra	tantric text dedicated to Lord Ganesha as the principal deity

Ganga	holy river in India
Ghee	clarified butter
Girija	Parvati or shakti
Gunas	qualities in the body
Hindu Trinity	Brahma, Vishnu, Shiva
Homa	offering oblations into the holy fire with mantras
Homa karma	sacrificial ceremony
Ida	pranic channel on the left side of the spine
Indriyas	organs of perception, instruments of mind
Ishana	an epithet of Shiva
Ishta devata	personal deity
Ishta mantra	personal mantra
Ishwara	the Supreme Soul, the ruler of the universe
Jagad	the universe
Jagadguru	guru of the universe, the Divine Mother
Japa	ritual repeated recitation of mantra
Japa mala	rosary
Jara	old age
Jiva	the individual soul
Jiva tattva	principle of the individual
Jiva-shiva-milana	union between *kundalini shakti* with *parama shiva*
Jñana	first step of prajna, acquisition of spiritual knowledge
Jñana kanda	the path of knowledge
Jñana pada	path of Self knowledge
Jñanam	knowledge, wisdom
Kala	principle of time, death, the lord of death
Kali	one of the names of the Divine Mother
Kara mala	counting of mantras with the fingers as rosary
Karma	action, duty, the law of cause and effect

Karma kanda	the path of action
Kartikeya	son of Lord Shiva and Parvati
Kaula chara	practice according to Kaulas, a tantric ritual
Khechari mudra	tongue pointed towards the fontanel
Koham	"Who Am I?"
Kriya pada	path of spiritual practice
Ksha	the last letter in Sanskrit alphabet
Kshiti	earth element in the body
Kulam	energy
Kundalini	latent spiritual energy in a person
Laya	dissolution
Lord Parama Shiva Bhattaraka	the master of 18 *vidyas*
Loukiki	traditional
Madhyama	intermittent thought process, middle
Mahabharata	the great epic scripture of India authored by Sage Vyasa, comprising the Gita
Mahamaya	power
Maheshwara	the supreme Lord
Mahi	earth
Mana	mind
Mangalya	auspiciousness
Manipura chakra	lumbar center
Mantra	holy syllable or prayer
Mantra chaitanya	awaking consciousness through a mantra
Mantra shastra	the science of mantra
Mantra vidya	the science how to use a mantra
Mathitva	churning milk or yogurt
Maya	the basis of creation, sustenance and dissolution, illusion
Merudanda	spine
Mimamsa	investigation, deep reflection, a branch of Indian Classical Philosophy
Moksha	liberation, the final goal of life in

Hinduism

Mount Kailasha in the Himalayas the abode of Lord Shiva, a place of pilgrimage for the Hindus

Mudra	position of body and hands
Muladhara chakra	coccyx center
Nada	the first primordial sound
Nadabrahma	a sound symbol of the Brahman
Nadi	energy channel, pranic channel in the spine
Navakula	nine aspects of life
Neem tree (margosa)	holy tree in India
Nigama	The Vedas
Nihilists	Buddhists, who believe that nothingness leads to the state of final emancipation or enlightenment
Nimitti karana	efficient cause
Niranajana	Formless, Brahman
Nirguna parameshvara	God without attributes
Nirvana	liberation in Buddhism
Niti Shastra	scriptures on values, morality, and ethics
Omkara	the letter a u m
Pada	step, the pillars, foot
Padma	lotus, chakra
Pancha devata puja	the five principal deities, Ganesha, Durga, Surya, Vishnu, and Shiva
Panchavati	five holy trees of the Hindus
Panchabhutas	five elements
Panditah	scholars in scriptures
Papa	sin
Papakarma	sinful actions
Para	supreme
Para vidya	supreme knowledge, supreme spiritual wisdom
Parabindu	upper point
Parama guru	superior guru
Paramashiva	the Supreme Shiva, unity with the

	Supreme Self
Paramatma	supreme soul
Paramesthi guru	absolute guru
Paramtattva	the supreme principle
Paranada	un-manifested sound or vibration
Parapara guru	supreme guru
Paravidya	supreme knowledge
Parvati	the divine consort of Lord Shiva and his worthy disciple
Pashyanti	cognition, the second aspect of sexual principle
Patala	nether-land one of the several levels of lower planes of existence
Pingala	pranic channel on the right side of the spine
Prajña or prajñana	wisdom
Prakriti	material cause, nature
Prakriti tattva	principle of nature
Prana	the vital breath, vital air, primal energy, life force
Pranayama	breath regulation, special breathing techniques
Prasad	consecrated food, food offered in the temple
Prayaga raj	the royal confluence of the three holy rivers, a place in North India known as Allahbad
Puja	ritual of worship, adoration
Punya	merits, virtues, noble deeds
Purana	mythological books in India composed by Sage Vyasa
Puranas	scriptures composed by Sage Vyasa
Purascarana	a special practice of Japa
Purusha	Brahman, the indwelling spirit

Puruvamimamsa	a branch of Indian Philosophy
Rajasic	a quality of restlessness and activities in human beings
Ramayana	scripture narrating the life and activities of Lord Rama
Ravi	sun
Rig Veda	one of the four Vedas
Rudra	epithet of Shiva
Sadhaka	spiritual aspirant, seeker
Sadhana	spiritual practice
Sadhana shastra	practical spiritual texts
Saguna parameshvara	God with attributes
Sahasrara chakra	fontanel, crown of the head
Sahitya	literature
Sakara	with form and attributes
Sama Veda	one of the four Vedas
Samadhi	state of communion with God, realization, superconscious state
Samkhya	scripture of Tantra
Sandhya	evening ritual
Sapta dhatus	seven ingredients or essences in the human body
Sarasvati	the third holy river in India (invisible)
Sarga	the process of creation
Sarva devata	all deities
Sashi	moon
Sat-Cit-Ananda	a name of the Supreme God, existence-consciousness-bliss
Sattvic	a quality of calmness in human beings
Sattvika jñana	pure knowledge
Saukhyam	state of happiness
Saumya	lunar, peace, beautiful one
Saura	solar, related to the sun
Shadanga	the six limbs or auxiliaries of the Vedas

Shaivachara	practice centered on Lord Shiva
Shaktah	worshipper of the Divine Mother
Shakti (Parvati)	the creative power of Brahman, divine energy, Divine Mother
Shambhavi mudra or vidya	open-eyed meditation, wisdom of Shiva
Shastra	scripture
Shiva	God as destroyer, the third Lord of the Hindu Trinity
Shunya	vacuum, space, sky, nothingness
Siddhantachara	path of contemplation and meditation
Siddhi	perfection and revelation
Sishya	disciple, follower
Smruti	Code of Law, memory
Spanda	the throb, vibration
Srishti	creation (vibration or energy)
Sukha	happiness
Surya	sun god
Sushumna	the central channel in the spine
Svadhisthana chakra	sacral center
Tamasic	the quality of inertia and laziness in a person
Tantra	a system of spiritual practice
Tantrika mantra	mantras used in tantric practice
Tapa	penance, austerity, self-mortification
Tattvas	principles or elements
Tattviki	metaphorical language in literature
Teertha	divine qualities, a holy place
Teja	fire principle
Thirta	holy place of pilgrimage
Toya	water
Triveni sangama	the confluence of the three holy rivers, the Ganga, Yamuna, and Saraswati
Upadana karana	material cause
Upadesha	initiation, teaching, instruction
Upanishads	the last part of the Vedas, also Vedanta
Uttarakhanda	a region in the Himalayas

Vaikhari	the spoken audible word
Vaishnavachara	practice centered on Lord Vishnu
Vakya	words, statements
Vamachara	a special tantric practice
Vasudeva	epithet of Vishnu
Vayu	the breath, air, prana, god of air/wind
Vedachara	vedic practice
Vedanta	Upanishads, a branch of Indian Philosophy
Vedas	the most ancient and holy scriptures of the Hindus
Vidya	knowledge
Vijakshara	root and seed mantra
Vijnana	second step of *prajna*, applied knowledge, science
Vimarsha	deliberation and discussion
Vinasha	destruction, dissolution
Virya	creative force, semen
Visarjan	withdrawal of the life-principle, dissolution, immersion
Vishnu	God as sustainer, the second God of the Hindu Trinity
Vishuddha chakra	cervical center
Vishvasa	the worshippers of Lord Vishnu
Vyakta	the manifested form, manifestation of God
Yajur Veda	one of the four Vedas
Yamuna	holy river in India
Yantra	geometrical shape used in tantric practices and rituals
Yoga	a branch of Indian Philosophy, esoteric meditation
Yogapada	art of self-discipline
Yoga Sutras of Patañjali	aphorisms on yoga as described by Sage Patañjali

About the Author

Paramahamsa Prajnanananda, the current head of the Kriya institutions started by Paramahamsa Hariharananda, has taken on his Master's mission of bringing the ancient secret teachings within the reach of common people who are thirsting for spiritual knowledge. Paramahamsa Prajnanananda was born in 1960 in the village of Pattamundai in Orissa, India. He has always been a sincere seeker of truth. After a childhood filled with prayer and a youth enriched by education joined with meditation, the former Triloki Dash became a caring teacher as a professor of Economics and guided and inspired many of his students spiritually.

As a college student, through an unquenchable thirst for God, he met many saints and visited many ashrams in the Himalayas, looking for a spiritual guide. While still a student, he met his master Paramahamsa Hariharananda, who initiated him into the path of Kriya Yoga. Brahmachari Triloki Dash was later initiated into the glorious path of *Sannyas* by his master, becoming Swami Prajnanananda Giri. On August 10, 1998, on his 39th birthday, the title of Paramahamsa, the highest title reserved for monks who attain the summit of realization, who are inspired and divine teachers, guides and saints, was conferred upon him by his loving and divine master Paramahamsa Hariharananda.

A truly powerful and extremely loving teacher, author and speaker on world religion, well versed in the scriptures of the East and West, he combines a divine compassion for humanity with his love for God and his mastery of complex philosophical thoughts. His vast knowledge and his oratory and intellectual skills are fully utilized in interpreting deep philosophical thoughts in the light of modern science and psychology. His metaphorical interpretation of the scriptures is very unique. Using Kriya Yoga as a reference point and an interpretative tool, Prajnananandaji manages to reveal the hidden truths contained in the most complex passages of the sacred texts in ways which make the meanings relevant and helpful in our daily lives.

With thought-provoking statements and revelatory explanations, quotations from the Bible and the Bhagavad Gita, and incidents from the lives of great souls, Paramahamsa Prajnanananda distils the wisdom of the ages into clear, relevant instructions on leading a moral and spiritual life in the world today. Without being overly pedantic, yet incorporating the texts of countless scriptures within his lectures, Paramahamsa Prajnanandaji does what most religious teachers stop short of doing and what most of us are thirsting for: he gives step by step methods for achieving self-realization. Gearing his lectures to the modern world of East and West, peppering them with colourful anecdotes, in his humorous yet compassionate style, with constant words of encouragement to those who must continue to live in the world, he guides disciples with the love of a mother. To those who are baffled by the vastness of ancient scriptural wisdom, the clear, concise and immensely helpful hints and guidance he provides, helps to make sense of book learning.

The power of his teachings lies in their simplicity and direct relevance to our lives. He teaches one of the simplest truths of the scriptures. One needs not only the desire for salvation, but also the guidance of the Guru and the regular practice of meditation and then and only then comes realization.

Paramahamsa Prajnanananda teaches only one lesson: the lesson of love. Through not only the study of scriptures, and the practice of meditation, but through every action and every breath, he urges us to realize that we are all divine and to achieve that blissful state of divine love and contentment, through basic self-discipline and the practice of simple *yogic* principles.

His loving guidance and deep compassion have won him the devotion and faith of countless disciples around the world whose lives he has transformed.

AVAILABLE BOOKS ON YOGA, PHILOSOPHY AND SPIRITUALITY

by Paramahamsa Hariharananda

Kriya Yoga ISBN 81-86713-05-0

Bhagavad Gita in the Light of Kriya Yoga, Volume I: ISBN 0-9639107-0-1, Volume II: ISBN 0-9639107-1-X, Volume III: ISBN 0-9639107-2-8

Isha Upanishad

by Paramahamsa Prajnanananda

Mahavatar Babaji: The Eternal Light of God, ISBN 81-86713-06-9

Lahiri Mahasaya: Fountainhead of Kriya Yoga, ISBN 3-901665-22-6

Swami Shriyukteshwar: Incarnation of Wisdom, ISBN 3-901665-23-4

Paramahamsa Hariharananda: River of Compassion, ISBN 3-901665-24-2

The Lineage of Kriya Yoga Masters ISBN 3-902038-13-6

My Time with the Master, ISBN 3-902038-08-X

Discourses on the Bhagavad Gita, Volume I, ISBN 3-901665-25-0, Volume II, ISBN 3-901665-26-9

The Torah, The Bible and Kriya Yoga, ISBN 81-86713-00-X

The Universe Within, ISBN 3-902038-14-4

Yoga: Pathway to the Divine, ISBN 3-901665-21-8

The Path of Love, ISBN 3-902038-07-1

Life and Values, ISBN 3-902038-09-8

Aksara Tattva, ISBN 81-87825-02-2

Nava Durga: The Multiple Forms of the Mother ISBN 3-901665-28-5

Nectar Drops: Sayings of Paramahamsa Hariharananda ISBN 3-901665-01-3

Words of Wisdom: Stories and Parables of Paramahamsa Hariharananda, ISBN 3-901665-00-5

Krishna Katha, ISBN 1-931733-00-7

A Successful Lifestyle, ISBN 1-931733-03-1

Daily Prayers, ISBN 1-931733-02-3

The Changing Nature of Relationships, ISBN 3-902038-10-1

Prapanna Gita, ISBN 1-971733-01-5

Daily Reflections, ISBN 3-902038-12-8

Gautama Buddha, ISBN 3-902038-16-0

The Body's Dance The Soul's Play, ISBN 3-902038-17-9

Jnana Sankalini Tantra, PB ISBN 3-902038-18-7, HB 3-902038-20-9

KRIYA YOGA

Kriya Yoga is a direct gift from God. The modern revival of Kriya Yoga began in 1861 by Mahavatar Babaji and has been handed down to this day through the master-disciple method of teaching.

Most of us live with a conception of God as omnipotent, omnipresent and almighty, but few are searching for God within ourselves. More so, we do not feel the living presence of God within us through our daily chores and duties. Kriya Yoga can make us feel the living presence of God through breath-control and meditation. Any work, *kri,* is done by *ya*, the indwelling soul.

The modern revival of this technique has brought ancient secret teachings within the reach of householders and families who are searching for lasting peace and happiness, and who are hungry to know God. This form of meditation can be added to enhance one's religious and spiritual practice.

KRIYA YOGA CONTACTS

USA
Kriya Yoga Institute
24757 SW 167th Avenue
P.O. Box 924615
Homestead, FL 33092-4615
Tel: +1 305 2471960
Fax: +1 305 2481951
E-mail: institute@kriya.org
www.kriya.org

INDIA
Hariharananda Gurukulam
Balighai
Puri 750002
Orissa
Tel/Fax: +0091 6752 246644
Tel/Fax: +0091 6752 246788
E-mail: pmission@sify.com
www.prajnanamission.org

EUROPE

Kriya Yoga Centre Vienna
Pottendorferstrasse 69
A-2523 Tattendorf Austria
Tel: +1 43 2253 81491
Fax: +1 43 2253 80462
E-mail: kriya.yoga.centre@aon.at
www.kriyayoga-europe.org

Kriya Yoga Centrum
Heezerweg 7
NL-6029 PP, Sterksel
The Netherlands
Tel: +31 40 2265576
Fax: +31 40 2265612
E-mail: kriya.yoga@worldonline.nl